A Creative Approach to the Classical Progymnasmata

Writing & Rhetoric

Book 3: Narrative II

Teacher's Edition

Paul Kortepeter

Writing & Rhetoric Book 3: Narrative II Teacher's Edition
© Classical Academic Press®, 2014
Version 1.1

Classical Academic Press
515 S. 32nd Street
Camp Hill, PA 17011

www.ClassicalAcademicPress.com

ISBN: 978-1-60051-236-0

Series content editor: Christine Perrin
Series editor: Gretchen Nesbit
Illustrations: Jason Rayner
Book design: Lenora Riley
Speech bubble icon courtesy of frankdesign/Vecteezy.com.
p. 67, Mask of Agamemnon image courtesy of Rosemania via wikipedia.com.
p. 105, Gaius Julius Caesar bust image courtesy of Andrew Bossi via wikipedia.com.
p. 178, Invasions of the Roman Empire map image courtesy of MapMaster via wikipedia.com.

BB.05.21

Narrative II

TABLE OF CONTENTS

A Typical Teaching Week

Veteran teachers know that rarely is there anything typical about a teaching week. These guidelines are intended to help bring some predictability to lesson planning. Although the parts of speech and other elements of grammar are important aspects of this course, its primary focus is writing and rhetoric—as the name implies. It is recommended that teachers alternate between a course in grammar one week and *Writing & Rhetoric: Narrative II* the next week. The schedule includes four days so that you can have flexibility to spend more time on some sections or to catch up.

All teachers have time constraints. Please note that you may not want to tackle summary, amplification, and other writing exercises all in one lesson. These options are provided so that you have ample choice to decide what your class should practice. There will be other opportunities to summarize, amplify, and write creatively in lessons to come. Each of these skills is important in developing a solid foundation for rhetoric.

Day One

1. The teacher models fluency by reading the text aloud while students follow along silently.

2. Students break off into pairs and reread the text to each other. In the case of longer stories, students can read in sections. Encouragement should be given to students to read with drama and flair where appropriate.

3. "Tell It Back" (Narration) and "Talk About It" should immediately follow the reading of the text while the story is still fresh in the students' minds. "Talk About It" is designed to help students analyze the meaning of texts and to see analogous situations, both in the world and in their own lives. Narration, the process of "telling back," can be done in pairs or by selecting individuals to narrate to the entire class. Playacting the story from memory is another possible form of narration. (Note: Solo students can tell back the story into a recording device or to an instructor.) The process of narration is intended to improve comprehension and long-term memory.

4. "Go Deeper" comprehension exercises follow each text. They can help students better understand the selection as they work with vocabulary, main ideas, and character traits.

Day Two

1. Optional: The teacher can appoint a student or the entire class to read the text again.

2. Students then work with the text through the "Writing Time" exercises. In ancient times, at this level, the primary exercise was to summarize or amplify the narrative. Other exercises include emulating a particular sentence, changing part of a story, or writing an entirely new story. Student work need not be completely original, but it should show some effort of thought. You may want more than one day for this step.

Day Three or Four*

1. A time of sharing work can wrap up each lesson. In order to build confidence and ability in public speaking, students should be encouraged to read their work aloud—either in pairs or to the entire class (or cohort).

2. The "Speak It" section creates opportunities for students to recite, to playact, and to share their work aloud. Please consider using a recording device whenever it would suit the situation. In this case, have the student listen back to her recording to get an idea of what sounded right and what could be improved. Have students read the elocution instructions at the end of the book to help them work on skill in presentation.

3. At this level, teachers should be giving feedback to students and requesting rewrites whenever feasible. The art of writing is rewriting. Most students do not self-edit well at this age or provide useful feedback to each other. As the child gets older, self-editing checklists will be provided within the Writing & Rhetoric course.

*The number of days per week assigned to the lessons is four so that you have some flexibility according to the pace and level of depth that you can take advantage of with your students.

Introduction to Students

Hello and How Do You Do?

Pleased to meet you, I'm sure. Or perhaps we have already met in the first two books of this series: *Fable* and *Narrative I*. If so, I'm very glad that you are back in action! This time around you will stuff some new and wonderful stories into your cranium (that is, your skull!), and these stories are more interesting than ever before. You will get even better at understanding how stories are made by listening to them, narrating them, playing with word choice, outlining, highlighting, summarizing, and amplifying. Phew! And if that's not enough, you'll also learn the difference between fact and opinion, fiction and nonfiction. No extra charge! You will also be developing your skills as a writer.

Two things will never fail to help you with your writing: First, you should read a lot. Turn off the TV, drop the video game controller, and read! Reading is the painless way to learn to write. You will absorb good writing the way a sponge absorbs water. I don't know any really decent writer who doesn't dedicate a fair bit of time to reading. So get cozy with books and read, read, read! Second, you should practice writing stories by imitating the excellent stories you are hopefully reading. Practice makes perfect, as they say.

That's pretty much what these writing exercises are all about: reading and imitation. They are inspired by an ancient method of learning to write and speak known as the *progymnasmata*. "*Progymnasmata*?" you say. "Now that's a strange word." Well, of course it's strange! It's Greek, and Greek always sounds a little strange to English ears. *Progymnasmata* means "preliminary exercises." These exercises are fitness training for the writer in you, a writing workout before you study rhetoric. (Yikes, another Greek word!)

You can only be a good athlete if your body, through warm-ups and exercise, is strong, fit, and in shape. You can only be a good writer and speaker if you've mastered vocabulary, grammar, summary, amplification, and so on. Rhetoric is the game itself—football, soccer, basketball, figure skating, relay racing, and so on. The *progymnasmata* are the stretches, the warm-ups—the push-ups, sit-ups, leg lifts, and chin-ups—needed for you to become a good writer and speaker.

The *progymnasmata* (*progym*) follow a step-by-step guide to good writing created by two ancient teachers, Hermogenes and Apthonius. These two chaps lived in the Greek-speaking part of the Roman Empire, one in the city of Tarsus and the other in the city of Antioch. We'll take a look at their lives a little later. What you should know for now is that you are following a very ancient course of study that is still an excellent way to learn writing and speaking today, nearly 2,000 years after Hermogenes and Apthonius lived.

Reading and imitation. Imitation and reading. That's what the *progym* is all about. Happy writing!

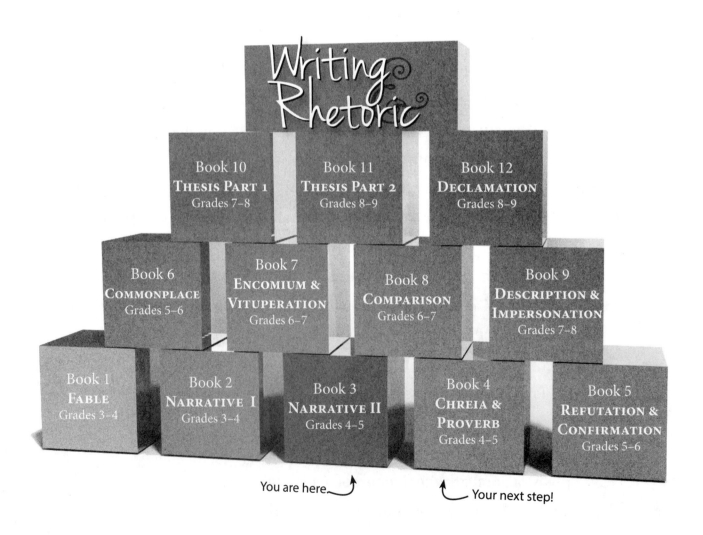

Introduction

Writing Happily

Where We Are Now with Writing

When it comes to writing, some students see the process as pure delight. That was my experience. I always loved taking a blank sheet of paper and transforming it into something magical: a carnival twinkling in the night, a city street shining with rain and reflecting gas lamps, an avalanche flying down a spire of rock. But I know that writing is not a magical world for many children or even some adults.

When I served as a writing instructor at the University of Southern California (USC), I saw firsthand the failure of writing instruction at our primary and secondary schools. Hardly a day went by that I wasn't grading a stack of papers, and the torment, the agony, of writing seemed to writhe through the pages.

Many of those college students had difficulty writing grammatically correct and coherent paragraphs—let alone entire essays, persuasively written. These were smart students from privileged backgrounds. So how did they get to college with such meager writing skills? What was happening in school or at home to sabotage the development of writing? Something was clearly not working.

Some years after teaching at USC, I helped to establish The Oaks Academy in the inner city of Indianapolis. Our school has grown from a modest 50 students in 1998 to 500-plus students today. At The Oaks, our mission is "to provide a rich, classical education to children of diverse racial and socioeconomic backgrounds." Our diversity includes children who grow up in highly involved families as well as children who have limited access to opportunity and must often fend for themselves academically.

As director of curriculum, I was determined to find a writing program that served the needs of all of our students. I wanted a program that combined the best modern practices with the principles of classical education as defined by such disparate educators as the Roman rhetorician Quintilian and nineteenth-century

British reformer Charlotte Mason. I felt strongly that students could be confident, persuasive writers by the eighth grade if they received the right combination of models and practice. Above all, I wanted to avoid the wasted years that led to faltering communication in college and beyond.

I examined quite a few programs. Each in its own way seemed to be lacking—both the modern courses and those purporting to be classically inspired. Nothing seemed to be "just right." Some programs were difficult to use. Others seemed too frivolous on the one hand or too heavy on the other. Still others lacked the necessary incremental steps.

The book you have in your hand is the fruit of my dissatisfaction. This is a curriculum built on the solid foundations of the past and framed with the vitality of the present. This is a curriculum that has been tested by ancient, medieval, and modern kids and has proven reliable for the ages. Along with caring teachers and a diet of good books, the Writing & Rhetoric series has taken the young people of The Oaks, kids from all sorts of advantaged and disadvantaged backgrounds, and shaped them into fine communicators. As a current eighth-grade teacher, I am often delighted by the rhetorical firepower in my classroom.

Imitation as a Foundation for Learning Writing

An examination of the theory and practice of modern composition reveals some obvious problems. Too often students are asked to brainstorm, "prewrite," or "free write" according to their personal interests. This means, in essence, that they are supposed to conjure ideas out of thin air. When faced with a blank piece of paper, many students naturally draw a blank. They lack a conversation in their heads about where to begin. Good writing requires content. It abhors a vacuum.

Students are also expected to write with no clear model before them. Modern composition scolds traditional writing instruction as rote and unimaginative. It takes imitation to task for a lack of freedom and personal expression. And yet effective communication from writer to reader always requires some sort of form and structure. Many of history's greatest writers learned by imitation. Benjamin Franklin, for example, taught himself to write by studying classic books and copying whole passages verbatim. He would then put the book aside and try to reconstruct the passage from memory.

Today's emphasis on originality and creativity has failed. When students lack a form by which to express their ideas, their creativity lacks vitality. As Alexander Pope tells us in his "An Essay on Criticism": "True Ease in Writing comes from Art, not Chance, / As those move easiest who have learn'd to dance." In other words, writing takes the same kind of determined study as ballet or diving. Creativity uses conventional form as a stage or a springboard from which to launch grand *jetés* and somersaults.

But there's yet another problem. Too often students are expected to tackle complex writing assignments without learning the necessary intermediate steps. Without the requisite scaffolding, teachers require summer vacation narratives, persuasive letters, research papers, and poetic descriptions. All of these forms require skills that must be developed in stages. The assumption is that because most everyone can speak English well enough to be understood and form letters with a pencil, that everyone should be able to write well. And yet how many of us would expect a child to sit at a piano, without piano lessons, and play a concerto? How many of us would expect a child with a hammer and a chisel and a block of marble to carve the statue of David as well as Michelangelo?

Writing is never automatic. The skills of the trade will not miraculously materialize somewhere along the school way. They take years to master. This is because writing demands thoughtfulness, organization, grammatical skill, rhetorical skill, and an ear for the English language. Most children have a natural inclination for one or two of these skills. Rarely do they have a knack for all. The other skills need to be developed and matured.

When it comes down to it, writing is simply thinking on paper (or thinking in some digital realm). Writing is thought translated to symbols—the symbolic language of the alphabet. The difficulty lies in the process of translation. I may picture a face or a waterfall clearly in my mind. It's quite another thing to describe the face or waterfall articulately in writing. I may have beautiful arguments on the tip of my tongue for buying a Great Dane puppy, but can I make the case persuasively on a piece of paper? The thinking comes first; the writing comes second. Both need to mature together.

What Is to Be Done?

If we have lost our way, it rarely helps to plunge blindly forward. It often helps to retrace our steps. And so it is with writing. We have much to learn from the wisdom of the ages. The Greeks developed a system of persuasive speaking known as rhetoric. The Romans, who came later, were also in love with rhetoric, but they took it to the next level. In order to prepare their young students for dazzling oration, the Romans invented a complementary system of persuasive writing.

This writing system was so dynamic, so effective, that it outlasted the Roman Empire, the Middle Ages, and the Renaissance. It even survived into early modern times. This method employed fluent reading, careful listening, models for imitation, and progressive steps. In short, it did many of the things that are out of fashion today, but gave us writers like Cicero and John Milton.

The Romans in the Greek-speaking part of the Empire called their system the *progymnasmata* (pro-gym-naz-ma-ta). This strange mouthful of a word derives from the same root for exercise as do "gymnasium" and "gymnastics." It means "preliminary exercises." The goal of these lessons is to prepare students for rhetoric, which is the art of writing well and speaking persuasively. This method assumes that students learn best by reading excellent examples of literature and by growing their skills through imitation. Successful writers study great writing. Successful orators study great speeches.

Each exercise is intended to impart a skill (or tool) that can be employed in all kinds of writing and speaking. The exercises are arranged from simple to more complex. What's more, the exercises are cumulative, meaning that later exercises incorporate the skills acquired in preceding exercises. This means, for example, that the skill of reporting or narrating (derived from the narrative exercise) will be regularly practiced and used in future exercises. While engaged in praising an individual (encomium exercise), a student will need to report or narrate an important event or achievement. While comparing two individuals (comparison exercise), a student will often need to praise one of those individuals (encomium).

Studying and acquiring the skills imparted by the *progymnasmata* (hereafter referred to as *progym*) exercises is much like the way in which we acquire skill in cooking or in a sport such as soccer. In the case of cooking, students must first learn the foundational skills of measuring, pouring, and mixing. Then they must learn skills relating to using a frying pan and oven. Each recipe requires the employment of these foundational skills—no matter how complicated it is. A sport like soccer also requires the mastery of basic skills such as kicking, passing, and dribbling. These foundational skills are carried forward into every soccer play and every game strategy.

Think of the *progym* as a step-by-step apprenticeship in the art of writing and rhetoric. What is an apprentice? It is a young person who is learning a skill from a master teacher. Our students will serve as apprentices to the great writers and great stories of history.

Quintilian, one of the master teachers of Rome, tells us that good habits are the foundation of education. In his *Institutio Oratoria*, he writes, "Once a bad habit has become ingrained, it is easier to break than bend. So strong is custom formed in early years." This master teacher also tells us that natural ability is nothing if it is not "cultivated by skillful teaching, persistent study, and continuous and extensive practice in writing, reading, and speaking."

Getting Started

The place to begin is reading, which should be encouraged as one of life's great pleasures from a child's earliest days. Parents should introduce books to babies as soon as they can keep their eyes open. Babies love to hear the sound of their parents' voices. They love the feeling of snuggling in a parent's lap. They love bright books and pictures. Reading helps develop joint attention (two people focusing at the same time on an object), which is necessary for any language acquisition. The more a child reads and is read to, the better the foundation for writing. And if a parent feels he or she has been negligent in reading, it's never too late to get started.

The necessary corollary is that we must limit screens: TV, the Internet, and video games should stay off as much as possible! Without realizing it, many parents sabotage the ability of their children to think by allowing an excess of these media. Researchers are telling us, in no uncertain terms, that an imbalance of electronics can be harmful to clear thinking and focused attention. If children don't have time for books, they don't have time for glowing screens. (Unless, of course, that glowing screen contains a book.) Even boredom and daydreaming can be more productive than too much media exposure! A brain needs rest in order to do the hard work of synthesizing information, problem solving, and making connections between ideas.

In addition to reading, it's important for children to get comfortable with the formation of letters. Children should work on penmanship to strengthen neural pathways that allow thinking and writing at the same time. Once writing mechanics come easily, it is much easier to make progress in the complex skill of "thinking on paper." As is often the case, there's more to a fine motor skill than meets the eye. With writing, children must learn to grip the pencil properly, to move their arms and wrists smoothly, and to stay focused on the page. Keep practice sessions short, but frequent—about ten minutes a day for seven- and eight-year-olds.

Before children begin *Writing & Rhetoric: Narrative II* they should have covered the concepts in the previous two books. Many teachers and parents have begun older students with the *Fable* and *Narrative I* books and worked through them to gain the skills those books offer.

After This—Formal Rhetoric

The formal study of rhetoric will develop in students a solid theoretical understanding of rhetoric, helping them to better understand why and how to employ the skills they have acquired while studying these exercises. The Writing & Rhetoric series (twelve books in all) will prepare your students to enjoy transforming that blank sheet of paper into a spectacular view from atop the pinnacle of their own imagination.

Best Foot Forward

The *Progym* and the Practice of Modern Writing

Although the *progym* are an ancient method of approaching writing, they are extraordinarily relevant today. This is because modern composition owes almost everything to the *progym*. Modern writing borrows heavily from many of the *progym*'s various exercises. For example, modern stories are essentially unchanged from the ancient fable and narrative forms. Modern expository essays contain elements from the ancient *chreia*, the refutation/confirmation, and other *progym* exercises. Persuasive essays of today are basically the same as the ancient commonplace and thesis exercises. In this series, you can expect your students to grow in all forms of modern composition—narrative, expository, descriptive, and persuasive—while at the same time developing unique rhetorical muscle.

The *progym* cover many elements of a standard English and Language Arts curriculum. In *Narrative II* these include:

- Writing narratives to develop real or imagined experiences or events using effective technique, descriptive details, and clear event sequences
- Using dialogue and description to develop experiences and events or show the responses of characters to situations
- Asking and answering questions to demonstrate understanding of the text
- Summarizing the text
- Describing in depth a character, setting, or event in a story or drama, drawing on specific details in the text
- Determining the meaning of words and phrases as they are used in a text
- Comparing and contrasting the point of view from which different stories are narrated, including the difference between first- and third-person narrations

While these goals are certainly worthwhile, the *progym* derive their strength from the incremental and thorough development of each form of writing. The Writing & Rhetoric series does not skip from form to form and leave the others behind, but rather builds a solid foundation of mastery by blending the forms. For example, no expository essay can truly be effective without description. No persuasive essay can be convincing without narrative. All good narrative writing requires description, and all good persuasive writing requires expository elements. Not only do the *progym* demand strong organization, but they retain all of the power of classical rhetoric.

Here is how the *progym* develop each stage of modern composition:

1. Fable—Narrative

2. Narrative—Narrative with descriptive elements

3. *Chreia* & Proverb—Expository essay with narrative, descriptive, and persuasive elements

4. Refutation & Confirmation—Persuasive essay with narrative, descriptive, and expository elements

5. Commonplace—Persuasive essay with narrative, descriptive, and expository elements

6. Encomium & Vituperation—Persuasive essay with narrative, descriptive, and expository elements

7. Comparison—Comparative essay with narrative, descriptive, and expository elements

8. Description & Impersonation—Descriptive essays with narrative, expository, persuasive, and comparative elements

9. Thesis Part 1—Persuasive essay with narrative, descriptive, expository, and comparative elements

10. Thesis Part 2—Persuasive speech with narrative, descriptive, expository, and comparative elements, as well as the three rhetorical appeals

11. Declamation—Persuasive essay or speech that marshals all the elements of the *progym* and brings them to bear upon judicial matters

All of the *progym* exercises are incorporated into the twelve-book Writing & Rhetoric series.

Objectives for *Narrative II*

Here are some of the major objectives for the exercises found in each section of this book:
1. Expose students to different forms of narrative writing as well as culturally important examples.

2. Model fluent reading for students and give them practice reading short texts.

3. Strengthen working memory through dictation, thus improving storage and manipulation of information.

4. Increase understanding of the flexibility and copiousness of language through sentence manipulation.

5. Facilitate student interaction with well-written texts through question and answer and through exercises in summary and amplification.

6. Give students opportunities to creatively imitate sentences and narrative sections.

7. Deepen the concepts of plot (beginning, middle, and end), dialogue, and description.

8. Encourage students to create their own fables and narratives with solid guidelines.

9. Widely and regularly require students to think critically.

Teaching Narrative II to Students

Throughout their lives, students will be telling and re-telling all kinds of stories. What a delight to know that rhetoric—the best and most persuasive writing and speaking—contains plenty of stories! Narrative is an essential rhetorical skill that never goes out of fashion. By learning the art of narrative, students can become excellent storytellers themselves.

Most likely your students have been exposed to many types of narrative from an early age. They've heard everything from simple fables to more complex parables and histories. The idea that there are different story types should not be surprising to them, but it helps to articulate this idea. Genres multiply as students get older, and the brain stores best what it can classify.

As always, there is wisdom in the sequence of the *progymnasmata* (*progym*). By starting with imaginative fables and stories, students wade into writing and rhetoric without getting in over their heads. They move from the simple to a more complex version of what they already know. Since the *progym* are cumulative, students can move forward with confidence, mastering each step along the way and using all that they have mastered in each succeeding exercise.

Getting to Know This Book

Learning to write isn't as easy as making pie, but it is potentially just as pleasurable. In *Writing & Rhetoric: Narrative II*, we've teamed up a writer and an editor who love literature and who have worked to make this not only an effective exercise of the past but a relevant, user-friendly, delightful program for the present. What follows is a brief description of the template of this book, explaining not only the content of each section but also its purpose and benefits.

The Chapter Story

Each chapter has a story (or several) that is well told, lively, and wise and has a beginning, middle, and end. Part of the beauty of the Writing & Rhetoric series is the fact that it uses stories that are noteworthy in their own right. When a child cares about a character and what happens to him—when she gets wrapped up in the language—her delight helps her to think and write more enthusiastically. Well-told stories also populate your students' minds with rich content so they get to practice skills without also having to invent content. All of the stories in the book are recorded in a downloadable MP3 file so that your students can experience the pleasure of being read to and taking the story in through a different door.

Tell It Back—Narration

Every time a student hears a story in this book, he will also practice narrating the story back. Multiple intelligences—memory, sequence, main idea—are developed by this practice. In addition to exercising their executive functions, students will begin to internalize an outline of the material. Later in this book, when they learn outlining, they will discover that they are already equipped to complete the task. Some educational models have based their entire strategy on this important skill.

Talk About It and Speak It

These two sections mirror our conviction that writing, speaking, and thinking are critical skills that work together. Some educators believe that difficulties with writing stem from a lack of deeper thought. These books use comprehension, reading aloud, discussion, and even oral performance as ways to help students become critical thinkers according to the way their bodies (and brains) are made. These three abilities—writing, speaking, and thinking—practiced together strengthen each other.

Go Deeper

This section seeks to develop comprehension, not only of the story but of individual words, roots of words, parts of speech, synonyms, and analogies. The questions, rather than draining a story of its delight, make the experience more vivid and stimulate an appetite for catching details that guide the student not only to the story's meaning but to the pleasure of the story as well. In most of the lessons, you will find a few multiple-choice questions in the "Go Deeper" section. Although classically minded educators often eschew multiple-choice questions, they are nonetheless a universal assessment tool. They are used in this section of *Writing & Rhetoric: Narrative II* so that students gain familiarity with this type of test.

Writing Time

This aspect of the book is the most obvious! We give all kinds of practice, from dictation to sentence play (in which students imitate sentences and learn how many ways there are to construct a sentence) to *copia* to summary and amplification. *Copia* is Latin for "abundance" or "copiousness." It is a stretching exercise that teaches students to reach for new words to express variations of the same idea, allowing them to experience the joy of the abundance of language. Students eventually get the chance to write their own stories after months of working with excellent models.

Important Notes

Flexibility is built into the program.

We have crafted this book to be useful to students at different levels with different needs. Teachers can do some of the exercises aloud instead of having students write them. Students can write out answers to "Talk About It" questions if teachers would like for them to have more written work. Teachers can also have students work together to tackle parts of lessons that are difficult. For instance, teachers should feel free to shorten the length of dictations or write difficult words on the board. Education is personal, and one size does not fit all.

You do not need to tackle all writing exercises for every chapter.

All teachers have important objectives and time constraints. As such, you may not want to tackle all exercises in each lesson. Each time you see the indicated icon, you'll know that, because of the diverse exercises provided, you have many choices for class practice. There will be other opportunities to do similar exercises in lessons to come. So, while each skill is important in developing a solid foundation for rhetoric, there will be numerous opportunities for students to work on those skills. Teachers know their students best and you should feel free to choose your schedule accordingly.

Decide whether to do oral narration or outlining.

When you see the indicated icon, you should decide whether oral narration or narration via outline would best serve your class. Oral narration serves the memory, while outlining improves understanding of story structure. Doing both is also a fine choice. Again, we aim for you as the teacher to tailor this program to the needs of your students. We are working our way toward written narrations and several of these lessons contain the building blocks of written narration.

Consider using sentence suggestion.

For some students, content generating at this stage is still quite time consuming. When you come to an instruction that asks students to use a word they have just defined in a sentence (these instructions will be indicated with the icon you see above), consider giving them a prompt that helps them create a stronger sentence. For instance, if the instruction is, "Use the word 'conceited' in a sentence," you could prompt students by giving them examples of conceited people: movie stars or famous soccer players, etc. Instruct students to finish the sentence that you have begun.

Highlight.

Throughout this book, we teach the skill of highlighting to differentiate between the fictional or opinion parts of a piece and the nonfiction or fact parts. Sometimes these instructions sequentially follow the piece (on the next page, for instance). In the Teacher's Edition we include the highlighting and reference the instruction to the student. The student edition does not include the highlighting.

Include elocution instruction.

We believe that speaking well makes students better writers and that writing well makes for better speakers. We focus in this book on the various aspects of speaking well, which include recitations, speeches, dramatic presentation, and the sharing of student work. In each book we expand our elocution instructions. You will see them appear in chapter 1, and then we will prompt you in each "Speak It" section with an icon to remind you of the instructions. Check page 187 for a refresher on these instructions. Your students will need you to highlight one aspect or other of elocution every time they practice public speaking.

Lesson 1 ···············

What Makes a Story a Story?

People love stories, don't they? They love it when the movie theater grows dark or the curtain goes up at the theater or when they turn the first page of a book. People love the sense of new adventure that comes with the start of a story. Since people love stories, it only makes sense that you will be listened to, you will be heard better, if you can tell stories well.

Let's say you are the president of Eureka Bank and you want people to listen carefully to your speech about the importance of saving money in banks. "Saving money?" your listeners say. "Sounds about as interesting as watching paint dry." Yawn, yawn, *yawn*!

But then you tell the true story of a woman who threw out her mother's mattress. It was a moth-eaten, dusty old mattress, so why not get rid of it? Only after the mattress was hauled away by a garbage truck did the woman learn that it was stuffed with a million dollars. "A million dollars?" she screamed. Down the road she ran, looking high and low for the truck. In a panic, she searched through dumps and

1

landfills. Did she ever find the million-dollar mattress? No. The money is probably lying in a moldy heap under piles of rotten fish and blue cheese, lost forever.

Now you have your listeners' attention, don't you? No more yawning.

One of the reasons we study writing and speaking is to learn how to win people to our ideas. We want to persuade people that we have something important to share. The bank president wants to persuade people to save their money in his bank. The senator wants to persuade people to vote for her in the next election. And the boy on bended knee wants to persuade the girl to marry him.

The name for the art and practice of persuasive writing and speaking is an odd word called **rhetoric** (REH-teh-rik). Say it out loud a few times. Some people see rhetoric as an art just like painting or music. As with other arts, rhetoric is an ability that requires the long practice of skills and involves creativity in applying those skills. There is no one way to speak or write persuasively, no rule book or simple set of instructions. Just as there are many different ways for artists to portray a subject's face, rhetoric can be done an infinite number of ways and requires skill and creativity. And guess what? Storytelling is a huge part of rhetoric.

▶ What makes a story a story? Do you remember what every story has in common?
Every story has a beginning, a middle, and an end.

In other words, stories contain an order of events like a timeline. You've had some practice with timelines, haven't you? In a timeline of civilization, the ancient world is the beginning: ancient Egypt, ancient Babylon, ancient Greece, ancient Rome, ancient India, and so on. Then comes the middle of the story of civilization: the Middle Ages. This is the time of knights and castles, of barbarian invasions and far-off crusades, of queens and dukes and princesses. The end of the story of civilization, at least so far, is the modern age to which we belong.

A story contains its own timeline. Most stories start with the beginning, go to the middle, and finish at the end. But some stories start in the middle, go to the beginning, and finish at the end. And some stories actually start at the end and work backwards, finishing in the beginning. The stories in this book all follow the typical pattern: beginning, middle, and end.

If your life were a story, it might go like this: In the beginning you were a baby, sucking your thumb and slurping milk from a bottle. In the middle you were a toddler, a kid, a teenager, and finally an adult. At the end of your life story, you became an elderly person with a head of frosty hair. That is the story of every person who lives to see old age.

▶ Now think about the four seasons. If the seasons of the year were a story, what season might be the beginning?

> Poets often imagine the spring to be the youngest part of the year. It's the season when baby birds appear in their nests and baby lambs skip across their pastures.

▶ If the spring is the beginning of the year, what two seasons are the middle?

> Summer and fall. These seasons are the prime of the year, bright with color and ripe with fruit.

▶ What season does that leave to end the story?

> Winter! Poets often imagine the winter to be the old age of the year. Winter skies and winter snow appear as gray and white as the hair of an elderly person. Many animals sleep through the winter in hibernation. All of nature has the appearance of death.

But is winter the end of the story? No. Spring will wake the dead earth and the story of the years starts over again.

Taken together, the events of a story—the beginning, middle, and end—are called the **plot** of a story. "Plot" means "plan." Every story has a plan.

Besides having a plot, stories must also have **characters**. Think of any story and you will immediately think of the persons in the story. Lucy, Edmund, Aslan, and the White Witch are some of the characters in The Chronicles of Narnia. As you can see in the case of Aslan the lion, a character need not be a human being.

The characters of a story make the story interesting. How interesting would *Charlotte's Web* be without Charlotte? What if the author had written his book about an empty cobweb gathering dust on the ceiling? How interesting would "Hansel and Gretel" be without Hansel and Gretel? We want to see them escape the wicked, kid-eating witch. The persons of a story—the characters—make a story fun to read.

▶ Name some of the characters in "Little Red Riding Hood." Name some of the characters in the Chronicles of Narnia series or another popular book series.

> "Little Red Riding Hood": the wolf, Little Red Riding Hood, Grandmother, the hunter, the mother
> Chronicles of Narnia series: Aslan, Susan, Lucy, Edmund, Peter, Mr. Tumnus, Eustace, Jill, Prince Rillian, Mr. and Mrs. Beaver, to name a few

▶ Can you think of a story without characters? | No, there is no such thing. |

Now we know, after all is said and done, what makes a story a story. All narratives must have a beginning, a middle, and an end—a plot. They must also contain persons or characters.

Tell It Back—

TE 1. Everyone tells stories—your parents; your friends; your teachers; your pastors, priests, and rabbis; and even the president of the United States. Explain why it's important to be able to tell stories.

TE 2. What are the two central aspects that make a story?

Talk About It—

TE 1. Do you remember the definition of "rhetoric"? Use it properly in a sentence. What does it mean to persuade someone?

TE 2. Why is it important to speak persuasively if you are trying to sell cookies or lemonade? Why is it important to speak persuasively if someone says something untrue about you or your family?

TE 3. What are some things that make up the beginning, middle, and end of a year at school? What are some things that make up the beginning, middle, and end of a holiday such as Thanksgiving, Christmas, or Hanukkah?

TE 4. In the last book you learned that "narrative" is a fancy word for "story." To narrate means "to tell" and comes from the Latin word *narrare*, which also means "to tell." So if you're telling a story, you're narrating a narrative. Try using the words "narrate" and "narrative" correctly in two separate sentences.

Go Deeper—

A This exercise can be completed intuitively, but prior knowledge of the selected stories is helpful.

1. Almost every story has a beginning, a middle, and an end. Try to put the events in order below using *B* for beginning, *M* for middle, and *E* for end. There are clues in these passages to help you figure out the correct order. **A**

A. Little House in the Big Woods —based on the book (with the same name) by Laura Ingalls Wilder

___**B**___ In the black winter night, Ma and her daughter Laura go outside to milk the cow. They are surprised to see a dark shape by the wooden fence. Ma thinks it's her cow, Sukey, out of the barn.

___**M**___ Ma gives the cow a slap on the shoulder and tells her to get out of the way of the gate. But the lantern reveals long, shaggy hair and two glowing eyes.

___**E**___ Ma realizes that the cow is, in fact, a bear. She grabs her daughter and runs to safety in the cabin.

B. Charlie and the Chocolate Factory —based on the book (with the same name) by Roald Dahl

___**E**___ Charlie becomes the new owner of the Wonka Chocolate Factory. No longer a poor boy, Charlie is rich for the rest of his days.

___**M**___ With a coin he finds in the gutter, Charlie buys a chocolate bar. As he unwraps the bar, he sees a glint of gold foil. Lo and behold, it's a golden ticket, a prize-winning passport into the chocolate factory! He is one of five lucky children who get to take a tour of the chocolate factory.

___**B**___ Charlie Bucket lives near a large, mysterious chocolate factory. Because he is a poor boy, he can rarely afford to buy a chocolate bar. Instead, he sniffs the delicious odors that waft from behind the high walls surrounding the strange factory buildings within.

C. Narrative of the Life of Frederick Douglass —

adapted from the autobiography (with the same name) by Frederick Douglass

_B_ I was born into slavery near Hillsborough in Talbot County, Maryland. I have no accurate knowledge of my age, never having seen any record containing it. My mother and I were separated when I was but an infant—before I knew her as my mother.

_E_ On the third day of September 1838, I left my chains and succeeded in reaching New York. How did I feel when I found myself in a free state? It was a moment of the highest excitement I ever experienced.

_M_ The escape plan we finally concluded upon was to get a large canoe and paddle directly up the Chesapeake Bay. On our arrival at the head of the bay, a distance of seventy or eighty miles from where we lived, it was our idea to turn our canoe adrift and follow the guidance of the north star till we got beyond Maryland.

D. The Emperor's New Clothes —adapted from Hans Christian Andersen's story in *The Yellow Fairy Book*, edited by Andrew Lang

_M_ One day two impostors arrived who gave themselves out as weavers and said that they knew how to manufacture the most beautiful cloth imaginable. Not only were the texture and pattern uncommonly beautiful but the clothes were invisible to anyone who was not fit for his office or who was unpardonably stupid. "Those must indeed be splendid clothes," thought the emperor. "If I had them on I could find out which men in my kingdom are unfit for the offices they hold; I could distinguish the wise from the stupid! Yes, this cloth must be woven for me at once." And he gave both the impostors much money, so that they might begin their work.

_B_ Many years ago there lived an emperor who was so fond of new clothes that he spent all his money on them in order to be beautifully dressed. He did not care about his soldiers; he did not care about the theater.

Lesson 1: What Makes a Story a Story?

He only liked to go out walking to show off his new clothes. He had a coat for every hour of the day.

__ E __ So the emperor went along in the parade under the splendid canopy, and all the people in the streets and at the windows said, "How matchless are the emperor's new clothes! That train fastened to his dress, how beautifully it hangs!"

No one wished it to be noticed that he could see nothing, for then he would have been unfit for his office, or else very stupid. None of the emperor's clothes had met with such approval as these had.

"But he has nothing on!" said a little child at last.

2. After each selection write "narrative" or "non-narrative." Use your best guess.

Songs

Remember that narratives have a timeline of events (a plot) and characters.

A. Sweet Betsy from Pike

> Oh, don't you remember sweet Betsy from Pike,
> Who crossed the big mountains with her lover Ike,
> With two yoke of cattle, a large yellow dog,
> A tall Shanghai rooster and one spotted hog?

_____ narrative _____

B. Do Your Ears Hang Low? —Children's song

> Do your ears hang low?
> Do they wobble to and fro?
> Can you tie 'em in a knot?
> Can you tie 'em in a bow?
> Can you throw 'em o'er your shoulder
> Like a continental soldier?
> Do your ears hang low?

_____ non-narrative _____

C. Home on the Range —Brewster M. Higley

Home, home on the range,

Where the deer and the antelope play,

Where seldom is heard a discouraging word

And the skies are not cloudy all day.

_____ non-narrative _____

D. Oh, My Darling Clementine —American folk ballad

In a cavern, in a canyon,

Excavating for a mine

Dwelt a miner forty-niner,

And his daughter Clementine.

Drove the ducklings to the water

Ev'ry morning just at nine,

Hit her foot against a splinter,

Fell into the foaming brine.

_____ narrative _____

Poems

Remember that narratives have a timeline of events (a plot) and characters.

A. The Tiger —William Blake

Tiger, tiger, burning bright

In the forests of the night,

What immortal hand or eye

Could frame thy fearful symmetry?

_____ non-narrative _____

B. There was a little girl —Henry Wadsworth Longfellow

There was a little girl

   Who had a little curl

Lesson 1: *What Makes a Story a Story?*

Right in the middle of her forehead.

When she was good

She was very, very good,

But when she was bad she was horrid!

———— non-narrative **B** ————

C. Froggie Went A-Courtin' —Scottish Nursery Rhyme

Froggie, a-courting he did ride,

Sword and pistol by his side.

He rode up to Miss Mouse's door

Where he had never been before.

He took Miss Mouse upon his knee,

Said, "Miss Mouse, will you marry me?"

———— narrative ————

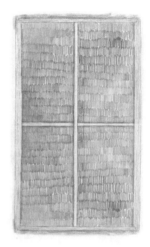

D. Limerick —often attributed to William Cosmo Monkhouse

There was a young lady from Niger,

Who smiled as she rode on a tiger.

They came back from the ride

With the lady inside,

And the smile on the face of the tiger.

———— narrative ————

E. For Want of a Nail —Proverbial rhyme

For want of a nail, the shoe was lost;

For want of the shoe, the horse was lost;

For want of the horse, the rider was lost;

For want of the rider, the battle was lost;

For want of the battle, the kingdom was lost;

And all from the want of a horseshoe nail.

———— non-narrative ————

Passages from Ancient Books

Remember that narratives have a timeline of events (a plot) and characters.

A. The Wandering Rocks —adapted from *Stories from the Odyssey*

A strong current caught the boat and whirled her swiftly towards danger. The water boiled and eddied around them, and the blinding spray was dashed into their faces. A sudden panic came upon the crew of the boat, so that they dropped their oars and sat helpless and unnerved, expecting instant death. In this emergency, Odysseus summoned up all his courage and strode up and down between the benches, shouting and calling each man by name. "Why are you sitting there," he cried, "huddled together like sheep? Row, men, row for your lives! And you, helmsman, steer straight for the passage, lest we be crushed between the Wandering Rocks."

_____ narrative _____

B. Daniel in the Lion's Den —Daniel 6:16-17 from the Hebrew Scriptures

So the king gave the order, and they brought Daniel and threw him into the lions' den. The king said to Daniel, "May your God, whom you serve continually, rescue you!" A stone was brought and placed over the mouth of the den, and the king sealed it with his own signet ring.

_____ narrative _____

C. Of David —Psalm 131:1-2 from the Hebrew Scriptures

My heart is not proud, O LORD, my eyes are not haughty; I do not concern myself with great matters or things too wonderful for me. But I have stilled and quieted my soul; like a weaned child with its mother, like a weaned child is my soul within me.

_____ non-narrative _____

Lesson 1: *What Makes a Story a Story?*

D. The Parable of the Lost Coin —Luke 15:8-9 from the Christian Scriptures

Or suppose a woman has ten silver coins and loses one. Does she not light a lamp, sweep the house and search carefully until she finds it? And when she finds it, she calls her friends and neighbors together and says, "Rejoice with me; I have found my lost coin."

_____ narrative _____

E. The Sayings of Confucius —adapted from a translation by Leonard Lyall

If a man doesn't care about beauty but honors worth, if he helps his father and mother with all of his strength, if he behaves modestly in public . . . and if he is faithful to his friends, then I would call that man wise, even if he has never been to school.

_____ non-narrative _____

F. Sun Tzu—The Art of War —adapted from a translation by Lionel Giles

After crossing a river, your army should get as far away from it as possible. If you must cross over a marsh, get over it as quickly as possible. All armies prefer high ground to low ground, and sunny places to dark.

_____ non-narrative _____

Writing Time— 🕐

1. **COPYWORK**—Neatly copy the sentence below in the space provided.

I was born into slavery near Hillsborough in Talbot County, Maryland. I have no accurate knowledge of my age, never having seen any record containing it.

_____

_____

_____

_____

2. **DICTATION**—Your teacher will read a little part of "Narrative of the Life of Frederick Douglass" back to you. Please listen carefully! After your teacher reads once, she will read slowly again and include the punctuation marks. Your task will be to write down the sentences as your teacher reads them one by one.

> Modify according to student level. Note that dictations are not spelling tests. Difficult words can be spelled on the board prior to dictation.
>
> How did I feel when I found myself in a free state? It was a moment of the highest excitement I ever experienced.

_____

3. **SUMMARY**—Write a summary narrative of one of your favorite stories. It can be as simple as a beginning, middle, and end, or you can elaborate further. Write it in complete sentences. Tell the name of the story as well as the major events and characters.

_____

_____

_____

_____

_____

_____

_____

_____

_____

_____

_____

Lesson 1: *What Makes a Story a Story?*

Speak It— 🎙️

c Remind your students that repetition is the key to memorizing anything. Consider breaking them up into groups and having each group put the information to music or chant, then have a competition to decide which one to adopt for the class.

Memorization is an important way to strengthen your brain and to add to its store of knowledge.**c**

Memorize your summary of the story you chose in the "Writing Time" section and share it with the class. Consider adding excitement and changing the volume of your voice according to the part of the story you are telling.

A Note on Proper Elocution

In the last two books in the Writing & Rhetoric series you learned about elocution, or the art of speaking skillfully. We believe that as you practice speaking skillfully, your writing will be improved. We also believe that your writing will improve your speaking—they work together.

Ancient educators taught us nearly everything we know about rhetoric. Aristotle noted two important parts of rhetoric: ***logos*** and ***lexis***. *Logos* is Greek for "word" and also for "logical reasoning." So *logos* is the content, the substance of a speech. It's what you put down on paper and the words that are spoken. *Lexis* is the delivery of the words, how the speech comes across to the audience.

Both *logos* and *lexis* are important for effective oration. We might call them substance and style today. The content of a speech can mean the difference between sharing excellent ideas or spouting stuff and nonsense. The way you use your voice in speaking can mean the difference between catching the interest of your audience or putting them to sleep.

What are some ways to make the delivery, or *lexis*, of a speech more interesting? You already know that proper volume—loudness and softness—is vital to *lexis*. Speed—not speaking too quickly or too slowly—is also key. In addition to proper volume and speed, there is also **inflection**. What is inflection?

Think about the different ways you could say the words, "I'd like to have you for dinner." If you say this sentence in a nice, casual voice, it sounds as if you are inviting someone to your house for a meal. If you say it sarcastically, it sounds like you really don't want them to come over for dinner. If you say it in a raspy, wolfish voice, it sounds as if you want to eat someone up. The change in the pitch or tone of your voice is called inflection.

In order to hold your audience's attention, you are going to need to use the highs and lows of your voice. Inflection tells the audience when they need to be excited or when they should laugh or get serious. We know that when a person asks us a question, his voice will get a little higher at the end of his sentence. We know when we're about to hear bad news because a person's voice goes lower. A good speaker will know how to use inflection to make his speech more powerful.

So when you practice speaking, remember to speak with

- clear pronunciation.
- good posture.
- eye contact.
- volume. Everyone in the room should be able to hear you.
- drama. You should sound sad when the words call for sorrow, angry when the words call for anger. Any emotion in the text should find its way into your voice.
- gestures. Gestures accentuate the emotions in your voice and make the reading even more dramatic.
- pauses and proper speed. Never read so quickly that you don't have a chance to take regular breaths. Pauses help to accentuate your emotions like gestures.

Lesson 1: What Makes a Story a Story?

Lesson 1: What Makes a Story a Story?

Tell It Back—

1. It is important to be able to tell stories because stories teach us about ourselves and our world. Everyone uses stories in their speech, and even whole groups of people—such as a nation—pass down stories and share them with each other. In America, for instance, we tell a lot of stories about Abraham Lincoln—how he learned to read and write on his own, how he boxed with bragging bullies, and how he walked miles to return some coins. These stories help to explain virtues—such as hard work, courage, and honesty—that Americans think are important for children to learn. Additionally, stories entertain us. In other words, stories can be just plain fun. They're good for our hearts and our happiness.

2. The two central aspects of a story are plot—beginning, middle, and end—and characters.

Talk About It—

1. Rhetoric is the practice (or art) of good writing and good speaking. Sample sentence: "People who learn rhetoric are often very persuasive." To persuade someone means to convince them that your ideas, opinions, or arguments are correct.

2. Any kind of salesperson must convince a shopper that his or her product is worth buying. A persuasive lemonade/cookie seller will talk about how delicious the lemonade and cookies are and tell stories about all the shoppers who enjoyed them. (Of course, it's important that the lemonade and cookies are truly delicious and that the stories are true. Rhetoric gets a bad name when persuasive people are not honest.)

   If someone is speaking dishonestly about you or your family, being able to speak well and persuasively would be very helpful to clear your name.

3. Answers will vary.

   ### School
   Beginning: Back to school night, orientation, new classrooms, new teachers
   Middle: Routine, homework, winter concert, winter break
   End: Field day, yearbook, graduation

   ### Holiday
   Beginning: Cleaning, shopping, cooking, pageants, crafts
   Middle: Family time, prayer, giving thanks, eating delicious food, exchanging gifts
   End: Feeling stuffed, long walks, cleaning, saying good-bye to out-of-town family

4. Sample sentences: I am going to narrate the story of "Little Red Riding Hood." In the oldest narrative of "Little Red Riding Hood," the girl is eaten by the wolf and is never rescued.

Notes

_____

_____

_____

_____

_____

_____

_____

_____

_____

_____

_____

_____

_____

_____

_____

_____

_____

_____

_____

The purpose of this lesson is to review various types of story (fable, parable, fairy tale, history, myth) and to introduce ballads (story songs).

In this lesson, your students will practice:
- distinguishing between story types based on simple definitions

Lesson 2

A Review of Narrative Types

In the first lesson, we learned that stories, or narratives, have two elements: a plot or plan with a beginning, middle, and end; and characters. People have been telling stories for so many thousands of years that different types of stories have come about. Let's review the types of stories you've encountered so far in the Writing & Rhetoric series: fables, parables, fairy tales, myths, and histories. Each of these story types has its own special definition.

A **fable** is a short story that teaches a simple moral lesson, usually with talking animals.

A **parable** is a short story that teaches a moral, spiritual, or heavenly lesson and is always true to life.

A **fairy tale** is a fanciful story for children, usually with magical people or creatures.

History is a narrative of actual events.

A **myth** is an ancient story not based on actual events, with gods, goddesses, and heroes, that is used to explain life and nature.

These are all good examples of types of stories, but there are still more. There are jokes, for instance. Do you realize that some of the funniest jokes contain a narrative? Here is a story joke from the Middle Ages:

A Spaniard was traveling late and desired to have a bed for the night. He came to a small town with a shabby little inn.

He rapped on the inn door, and a window opened above him. "What do you want?" demanded the innkeeper.

"For starters, I'd like some supper," the Spaniard replied.

"What's your name?" demanded the innkeeper.

"My name is Don Pedro Gonzales y Lopez Gayetan de Guevara."

"Well, sir," the innkeeper said, "We don't have enough meat for so many."

Why is this joke funny? It's because Spanish people are known to have long names. The lazy innkeeper is looking for an excuse to not cook supper and pretends that the one Spaniard is many people. This short joke contains a narrative; it has a beginning, a middle, and an end.

Another type of story is the **ballad**, a song that tells a story. Many ballads also contain a beginning, middle, and end. Here is the beginning of a very long ballad that tells the story of Robin Hood:

A Gest of Robin Hood

—adapted

Attend and listen, gentlemen,
That be of freeborn blood;
I shall tell you of a good yeoman,
His name was Robin Hood.

Robin was a proud outlaw,
While he walked upon the ground:
So courteous an outlaw
Was never another found.

Lesson 2: A Review of Narrative Types

The ballad goes on for nearly 2,000 lines more. We learn about Robin's many adventures as he battles the Sheriff of Nottingham. Sadly, the song ends with the betrayal and death of Robin Hood. The last stanza goes like this:

> Christ have mercy on his soul,
>
> That died upon the road!
>
> For he was a good outlaw,
>
> And did poor men much good.

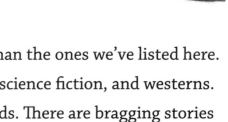

Of course, there are many more types of stories than the ones we've listed here. There are genre stories such as mysteries, romances, science fiction, and westerns. There are animal tales, folk tales, tall tales, and legends. There are bragging stories and tattling stories. There are biographies and autobiographies. There are as many types of stories in the world as are necessary to satisfy the human soul.

Tell It Back—

TE Take some time to memorize the story-type definitions in the Go Deeper section. Feel free to make notecards and practice with a partner. Then, describe in your own words each story type and give an example of it from this text or from your own experience.

Talk About It—

TE 1. Name one example of a story type that is not included in the list of categories you defined in your answer to the question in the "Tell It Back" section.

TE 2. Do you think that, in some way, the type of story you listed in question 1 does fit in one of the categories this chapter describes?

TE 3. Can you remember the title of a fable (animal tale) that you learned in *Writing & Rhetoric: Fable*?

Before you move ahead in this workbook, it might be a good idea to stop and have some practice playing story detective. So here's your job, young detective:

Using the definitions of the different types of narrative you've learned about so far, try to find clues that will help you to label the following short paragraphs. Here we go!

Go Deeper—

TE Each of these narratives represents a certain type of story. Label the following paragraphs as fable, parable, fairy tale, history, myth, or ballad.

Fable: A short story that teaches a simple moral lesson, usually with talking animals

Parable: A short story that teaches a moral, spiritual, or heavenly lesson and is always true to life

Fairy tale: A fanciful story for children, usually with magical people or creatures

History: A narrative of actual events

Myth: An ancient story not based on actual events, with gods, goddesses, and heroes, that is used to help explain life and nature

Ballad: A song that tells a story

A. ____fable____ In a field one summer's day a Grasshopper was hopping about, chirping and singing to its heart's content. An Ant passed by, bearing along a heavy kernel of corn he was taking to the nest. "Why not come and chat with me," said the Grasshopper, "instead of toiling and moiling in that way?" "I am helping to lay up food for the winter," said the Ant, "and recommend you do the same."

B. ____history____ Two days passed before the French army arrived. When King Philip saw the English his blood boiled, so much did he dislike them. He ordered his crossbowmen to advance, and the English sprang up to meet them. Just at that moment a terrible thunderstorm broke over the field, and the rain fell in torrents. The strings of the Frenchmen's bows were so drenched that they became almost useless.

Lesson 2: A Review of Narrative Types

C. ___myth___ Tyr the Brave stalked up to the wolf and thrust his arm into his enormous mouth. As soon as he did, the other gods bound the beast with the magic cords. When the wolf strained and pulled, the cords became tighter and stiffer. The gods shouted and laughed with glee when they saw that the wolf was bound. But Tyr did not join in their mirth, for the wolf in his rage snapped his great teeth together and bit off his hand.

D. ___fable___ A Fox was boasting to a Cat of its clever devices for escaping its enemies. "I have a whole bag of tricks," he said, "which contains a hundred ways of escaping my enemies." "I have only one," said the Cat. Just at that moment they heard the cry of a pack of hounds coming toward them. The Cat immediately scampered up a tree and hid. While the Fox was thinking about all the ways to escape his enemies, he was caught by the hounds and killed by the huntsmen.

E. ___parable___ He said: "In a certain town there was a judge who neither feared God nor cared about men. And there was a widow in that town who kept coming to him with the plea, 'Grant me justice against my adversary.' For some time he refused. But finally he said to himself, 'Even though I don't fear God or care about men, yet because this widow keeps bothering me, I will see that she gets justice, so that she won't eventually wear me out with her coming!'"

F. ___myth___ The three goddesses—Hera, Athena, and Aphrodite— appeared to the shepherd Paris while he was tending his sheep on Mount Ida. "Decide which of us is most beautiful," the goddesses demanded. Hera promised him power and riches if he chose her. Athena promised him glory and fame in war. But Aphrodite, goddess of love, knew the young man's heart. "If you choose me," she told Paris, "I will give you the most beautiful woman in the world."

G. _____ ballad _____

John Henry told his captain,

Lightning was in his eye:

"Captain, bet yo' last red cent on me,

For I'll beat it to the bottom or I'll die,

Lawd, Lawd, I'll beat it to the bottom or I'll die."

Sunshine hot and burning,

Weren't no breeze a-tall,

Sweat ran down like water down a hill,

That day John Henry let his hammer fall,

Lawd, Lawd, that day John Henry let his hammer fall.

H. _____ fairy tale _____ About midnight, the giant entered the apartment and with his club struck many blows on the bed, the very place that Jack had been sleeping. But Jack had put a log there in his place. Thinking that he had broken all Jack's bones, the giant went back to his room. Early the next morning, Jack put on a bold face and walked into the giant's room. "Thank you for my lodging," he said. "I slept very well!"

I. _____ fairy tale _____ A poor old woman, who lived with her one little grand-daughter in a wood, was out gathering sticks for fuel and found a green stalk of sugar cane. As she was about to add the cane to the bundle, along came a goblin in the form of a wild boar. "Give me the sugar cane," he snorted. But the old woman refused. "I am going to take the cane home and let my little granddaughter suck its sweet sap." The boar, angry at her refusal, said that during the coming night he would come and eat her granddaughter instead of the cane and went off into the wood.

J. _____ parable _____ Jesus replied: "A certain man was preparing a great banquet and invited many guests. At the time of the banquet he sent his servant to tell those who had been invited, 'Come, for everything is now

Lesson 2: A Review of Narrative Types

ready.' But they all alike began to make excuses. The first said, 'I have just bought a field, and I must go and see it. Please excuse me.' Another said, 'I have just bought five yoke of oxen, and I'm on my way to try them out. Please excuse me.' Still another said, 'I just got married, so I can't come.' The servant came back and reported this to his master. Then the owner of the house became angry and ordered his servant, 'Go out quickly into the streets and alleys of the town and bring in the poor, the crippled, the blind and the lame.'"

K. ___ ballad ___

Silvy, Silvy, all on one day,
She dressed herself in man's array,
A sword and pistol all by her side,
To meet her true love she did ride.

She met her true love all in the plain,
"Stand and deliver, kind sir," she said,
"Stand and deliver, kind sir," said she,
"Or else this moment you shall die."

Oh, when she'd robbed him of all his store,
She says, "Kind sir, there's one thing more,
A diamond ring which I know you have,
Deliver that, your sweet life to save."

L. ___ history ___ When Columbus discovered the New World he brought back with him to Europe many new and curious things, one of which was cocoa. Some years later, in 1519, the Spanish conquistador Cortes landed in Mexico, marched into the interior, and discovered, to his surprise, not the huts of savages but a beautiful city with palaces and museums. This city was the capital of the Aztecs, a remarkable people, notable alike for their ancient civilization and their wealth. Their national drink was chocolate, and Montezuma, their emperor, who lived in a state of luxurious magnificence, "took no other beverage than the *chocolatl*, a drink of chocolate flavored with vanilla and other spices."

Writing Time—

1. **COPYWORK**—Neatly copy the following sentence in the space provided: About midnight, the giant entered the apartment and with his club struck many blows on the bed, the very place that Jack had been sleeping.

_____

_____

_____

_____

2. **DICTATION**—Your teacher will read a little part of *Jack the Giant Killer* back to you. Please listen carefully! After your teacher reads once, she will read slowly again and include the punctuation marks. Your task will be to write down the sentences as your teacher reads them one by one.

> Modify according to student level. Note that dictations are not spelling tests. Difficult words can be spelled on the board prior to dictation.
>
> But Jack had put a log there in his place. Thinking that he had broken all Jack's bones, the giant went back to his room.

_____

_____

_____

_____

_____

3. **AMPLIFICATION**—Take the following small piece of a fairy tale and amplify it. Remember that when you amplify you can add description and details and further dialogue. In this case, because we are dealing with a fragment of a familiar story, you can also add some plot.

Jack the Giant Killer

—adapted from *Jack the Giant Killer* by Joseph Jacobs

About midnight, the giant entered the apartment and with his club struck many blows on the bed, the very place that Jack had been sleeping. But Jack had put a log there in his place. Thinking that he had broken all Jack's bones, the giant went back to his room. Early the next morning, Jack put on a bold face and walked into the giant's room. "Thank you for my lodging," he said. "I slept very well!"

_____

_____

_____

_____

_____

_____

_____

_____

_____

_____

_____

_____

_____

_____

_____

_____

_____

_____

_____

_____

_____

_____

_____

_____

_____

Speak It—

Choose one of the fragments from the "Go Deeper" section and memorize it. Referring to the elocution instructions found at the end of this book, prepare to share your selected piece with your class. Practice telling it with dramatic flair that will make those listening to you want to hear more of the story.

Lesson 2: A Review of Narrative Types

Tell It Back—

Answers will vary but should include the main ideas of the following definitions and an example of the story type:

Fable: a short story that teaches a simple moral lesson, usually with talking animals (Example: *The Frog and the Ox*)

Parable: a short story that teaches a moral, spiritual, or heavenly lesson and is always true to life (Example: *The Parable of the Lost Coin*)

Fairy tale: a fanciful story for children, usually with magical people or creatures (Example: *Jack the Giant Killer*)

History: a narrative of actual events (Example: *Barbarian Invasion Story*)

Myth: an ancient story not based on actual events, with gods, goddesses, and heroes, that is used to help explain life and nature (Example: *The Fifth Labor of Hercules*)

Ballad: a song that tells a story (Example: *A Gest of Robin Hood*)

Talk About It—

1. Answers will vary. Suggested answers include: mysteries, romances, science fiction, Westerns, animal tales, folk tales, tall tales, legends, bragging stories, tattling stories, biographies, and autobiographies.

2. Yes. For instance, autobiography and biography are types of history. Science fiction is a kind of future myth. Mysteries and romances could be parables if they contain a moral lesson. Each new form of story has something in common with an old form of story. There is a lot of variety but a lot of similarity when it comes to the basics of stories.

3. *The Lion and the Mouse*
   Three Young Bulls and a Lion
   The Crow and the Pitcher
   The Fox and the Grapes
   The Ass and His Driver
   The Mice in Council
   The Dog and Her Reflection
   The Shepherd Boy and the Wolf
   The Tale of the Chinese Farmer
   The Trees Choose a King
   The Ants and the Grasshopper

Go Deeper—

Here are the sources for the stories in this section:

A. —from *Aesop's Fables*

B. —from *Lord and Vassal: History Stories of Other Lands* by Arthur Guy Terry

C. —*Fenris Wolf, Stories from the Northern Sagas* edited by E.E. Speight and A.F. Major

D. —from *Aesop's Fables*

E. —Luke 18:2–5 from the Christian Scriptures

F. —from *Tales of the Trojan War* by Kamini Khanduri

G. —ballad by anonymous

H. —adapted from *Jack the Giant Killer* by Joseph Jacobs

I. —adapted from "A Dreadful Boar" in *Chinese Fairy Tales: Forty Stories Told by Almond-Eyed Folk* by Adele Fielde

J. —Luke 14:16–21 from the Christian Scriptures

K. —adapted from "The Lady Turned Highwayman"

L. —adapted from *Cocoa and Chocolate: Their History from Plantation to Consumer* by Arthur William Knapp

The purpose of this lesson is to refresh in the minds of your students the importance of fables and to remind students that the main idea of most fables is found in the moral.

In this lesson, your students will practice:
- finding synonyms for nouns and adjectives
- summarizing a fable
- amplifying a fable
- writing a fable
- proper elocution

Lesson 3 ·

Fable Refresher

Chances are that you already know about fables. They are one of the simplest forms of story, and the entire first book of the Writing & Rhetoric series is dedicated to them. Let's take a minute to review what you may have learned about fables in previous lessons.

For many hundreds of years, narratives have been used to teach valuable lessons to children. One type of narrative, fables, is one of the most enjoyable ways to learn to be a little wiser. It's much easier to hear a story about a foolish animal than to receive a lecture about not acting a fool yourself, isn't it? At the end of a fable, a moral lesson usually sums up the story. Here is a fable by the greatest of fable tellers, Aesop of ancient Greece.

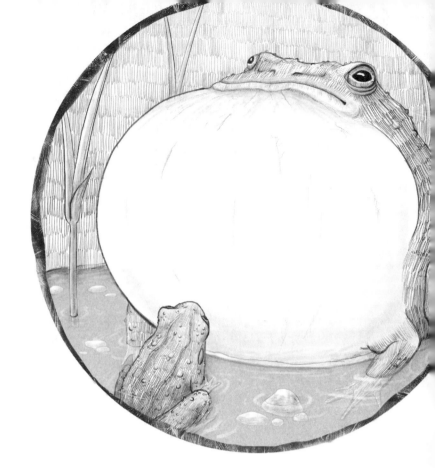

The Frog and the Ox

—*Aesop's Fables* (based on Joseph Jacobs's 1894 retelling)

"Oh, Father," said a little Frog to the big one sitting by the side of a pool, "I have seen such a terrible monster! It was as big as a mountain, with horns on its head, and a long tail, and it had hoofs divided in two."

"Tush, tush, tush," said the old Frog, "that was only the Farmer's Ox. It isn't so big either. He may be a little bit taller than I, but I could easily make myself as broad. Just you see!" So he blew himself out, and blew himself out, and blew himself out. "Was he as big as that?" asked the old Frog.

"Oh, much bigger than that," said the young Frog.

Again the old one blew himself out, and asked the young one if the Ox was as big as that.

"Bigger, Father, bigger," was the reply.

So the Frog took a deep breath, and blew and blew and blew, and swelled and swelled and swelled. And then he said: "I'm sure the Ox is not as big as—" But at that moment the **conceited** old Frog burst.

MORAL: *Self-conceit may lead to self-destruction.*

Lesson 3: *Fable Refresher*

Tell It Back—Narration

Without looking at the parable, tell back *The Frog and the Ox* as best as you can remember it using your own words and any words from the story. For further practice, you can record your telling back and play it afterward. Try to keep the events of the story in their proper order. Here is the first sentence to get you started: "'Oh, father,' said a little Frog to the big one sitting by the side of a pool, 'I have seen such a terrible monster!'"

Talk About It—

TE 1. The word "boast" comes from a German word meaning "to blow up, to puff up, to swell." Some typical boasting remarks are, "I can do that with my eyes closed," or "I can do that with one arm tied behind my back." Why do you suppose some people boast? What does the boaster hope to accomplish?

TE 2. What is another word for boasting?

TE 3. Julius Caesar fought a short war with the kingdom of Pontus in 47 BC. He arrived outside the town of Zela and was attacked by a huge army. Without budging, Julius Caesar's Roman forces swiftly defeated their enemies. The battle was such an easy victory that Caesar boasted in Latin, *"Veni, vidi, vici,"* which means "I came, I saw, I conquered." Why do you think Caesar said this? How is Caesar's boast different than the Frog's boast, "I could easily make myself just as broad as the Ox"?

TE 4. A proverb from the Hebrew Scriptures says, "Let someone else praise you, and not your own mouth; an outsider, and not your own lips" (Proverbs 27:2). Is this wise advice? Why or why not?

Go Deeper—

1. What proverb is most like the moral of *The Frog and the Ox*?

   a. Gray hair is a crown of splendor.

   b. A foolish son is his father's ruin.

   c. Pride goes before a fall.

   d. Little friends may prove great friends.

2. Circle the adjective that best describes the old Frog.

   humble   boasting   cowardly   courageous   super

3. Circle the object the old Frog is most like.

   a tuba   a balloon   an egg   a bar of soap   a firecracker

4. The old Frog bursts while trying to impress the young Frog. Why do you think it was important to the old Frog to appear as big as the Ox? Use complete sentences in your answer.

   The old Frog didn't want his son to think there was any animal bigger or better than him. _____

   _____

   _____

   _____

   _____

   _____

   _____

   _____

5. Look up the word "conceited" in a dictionary. Write the definition in the space below and then use "conceited" in your own complete sentence. Make sure that your sentence hints at the meaning of the word. In other words, another person should be able to guess at what "conceited" means because of your sentence.

Definition: To be conceited is to think too highly of oneself. _____

_____

_____

Sentence: The conceited movie star _____

Sample sentence: The conceited movie star blew kisses to her fans and then rolled her eyes.

_____

_____

_____

_____

_____ .

A complete sentence will have a subject and a verb, and it will express a complete thought. Always start with a capital letter. Always finish with an end mark such as a period or question mark.

6. Look up the word "conceited" in a thesaurus. Write down other words that are **synonyms** of "conceited." A synonym is a word that has nearly the same meaning.

Sample answers: big-headed, egotistical, cocky, snotty

_____

_____

7. Use a synonym of "conceited" to rewrite the sentence you wrote in #5 above.

Sample sentence: The big-headed movie star blew kisses to her fans and then rolled her eyes.

_____

_____

Writing Time— 🕐

1. **DICTATION**—Your teacher will read a little part of *The Frog and the Ox* back to you. Please listen carefully! After your teacher reads once, she will read slowly again and include the punctuation marks. Your task will be to write down the sentences as your teacher reads them one by one.

> Modify according to student level. Note that dictations are not spelling tests. Difficult words can be spelled on the board prior to dictation.
>
> 💬 He may be a little bit taller than I, but I could easily make myself as broad. Just you see!

_____

_____

2. **SENTENCE PLAY**—

   A. <u>So the Frog took a deep breath, and blew and blew and blew, and swelled and swelled and swelled.</u> What if the Frog didn't take a deep breath but instead shot out his tongue? The sentence might now read, <u>So the Frog shot out his tongue, and licked and licked and licked, and grinned and grinned and grinned.</u> Follow the same pattern in the following sentences by repeating **verbs**—the action words.

   i. What might happen if the Frog took a big jump?

   The Frog took a big jump and _____

   > Sample sentence: The Frog took a big jump and flipped and flipped and flipped, and crashed and crashed and crashed.

   _____.

   ii. What if the Frog started to sing?

   The Frog started to sing and _____

   > Sample sentence: The Frog started to sing and chirped and chirped and chirped, and croaked and croaked and croaked.

   _____.

B. <u>He may be a little bit taller than I, but I could easily make myself as broad.</u>

What a silly boast for a frog to make about an ox! Now it's your turn to write an equally conceited boast.

   i. Using the underlined sentence as a model, write a boast for a snail about a racehorse.

"She may be a little bit _____ than I, but I could easily _____."

> Sample sentence: She may be a little bit taller than I, but I could easily outrun her.

  ii. Using the underlined sentence as a model, write a boast for a beggar about a king.

"He may be a little bit _____ than I, but I could easily _____."

> Sample sentence: He may be a little bit better dressed than I, but I could easily buy a crown as nice as his.

 iii. Using the underlined sentence as a model, write your own boast for a mouse about a cat.

_____

_____

> Sample sentence: She may be a little bit sharper in the teeth than I, but I could easily wrestle her to the ground.

3. **COPIOUSNESS**—If you worked with the first books in the Writing & Rhetoric series (*Fable* and *Narrative I*), you are familiar with copious writing. Practicing copiousness means that you are going to find lots of ways to say the same thing. In the Writing and Rhetoric series, copiousness comes in the writing section of each lesson.[A]

[A] *Copia* is Latin for "abundance" or "copiousness." It is a stretching exercise for students of rhetoric, a method whereby students reach for new words to express variations of the same idea. The Dutch scholar Erasmus used copiousness as a method for training students in rhetoric during the sixteenth century. His book *De Utraque Verborum ac Rerum Copia* is famous for finding hundreds of variations for the statement, "Your letter pleased me greatly." Examples of these variations include: "Your epistle greatly raised my spirits," "Your missive filled me with much delight," and "What a joy it was to receive your letter." Erasmus's goal was to help his students grow in eloquence and in flexibility as they reworked sentences with the full array of words at their disposal.

Whether you know it or not, you speak copiously all the time. Take the typical kid who has ice cream on the brain. She may say, "Wow, it's hot. What about ice cream?" "I'm boiling. Ice cream sure sounds amazing." "I feel like I'm stuck in a furnace. I need ice cream." "I'm a puddle of sweat. I'll perish without ice cream." And so on. Copiousness comes naturally, especially when you want something really, really badly.

To begin this practice, you're going to work on changing the nouns and adjectives in a sentence.

A **noun** is a person, place, thing, or idea. An **adjective** adds description to a noun and helps us to "see" it more clearly. For example, when you sell cold lemonade, "lemonade" is a noun because it is a thing. The word "cold" is an adjective because it describes the lemonade. Here's another example: When you visit your "sweet, old grandmother," "grandmother" is a noun because it is a person. What are the adjectives that describe grandmother? There are two. sweet and old

A. Mark the nouns and adjectives in the following sentence. Place an *N* over the nouns and an *ADJ* over the adjectives. There are four nouns and three adjectives.

    N   ADJ N   ADJ N   ADJ   N

"Oh, Father," said a little Frog to the big Frog, "I have seen such a terrible monster!"

B. In the sentence you labeled, replace the adjectives with synonyms, or adjectives that have close to the same meaning. Do not repeat any words. Use a thesaurus only if you get stuck.

> Sample synonyms for "little": small, short, tiny, itsy-bitsy, mini, teeny, wee, puny, or (as implied by the story) younger or child (as in child frog)

   i. "Oh, Father," said a _____ Frog to

      the _____ Frog, "I have seen such a

      _____ monster!"

Lesson 3: Fable Refresher

ii. "Oh, Father," said a _____ Frog to

the _____ Frog, "I have seen such a

_____ monster!"

iii. "Oh, Father," said a _____ Frog to

the _____ Frog, "I have seen such a

_____ monster!"

Sample synonyms for "big": large, fat, huge, gross, enormous, or (as implied by the story) older or adult

Sample synonyms for "terrible": awful, horrendous, fearful, frightening, shocking, dreadful

C. Next replace the nouns "father" and "monster" with synonyms, or nouns that have close to the same meaning. Do not repeat any words. Use a thesaurus only if you get stuck.

Sample synonyms for father: papa, dad, daddy, pa, pop

i. "Oh, _____," said a little Frog to the big Frog, "I have

seen such a terrible _____!"

Sample synonyms for monster: beast, brute, creature, giant, freak

ii. "Oh, _____," said a little Frog to the big Frog, "I have

seen such a terrible _____!"

Now replace both the adjectives and nouns (except for "Frog") with any adjectives or nouns you'd like. They do not have to be synonyms. Do not repeat any words that you have already used.

iii. "Oh, _____," said a _____ Frog
         (N)   (ADJ)

to the _____ Frog, "I have seen such a
        (ADJ)

_____ _____!"
   (ADJ)   (N)

Sample sentence: "Oh, Cousin, said a green Frog to the red Frog, I have seen such a crazy dragonfly!"

iv. "Oh, _____," said a _____ Frog
             (N)   (ADJ)

to the _____ Frog, "I have seen such a
              (ADJ)

_____ _____ !"
      (ADJ)   (N)

D. Can you think of a noun to replace the word "frog" that has nearly the same meaning? Hint: You can be creative and use a word that describes a frog, such as "jumper."

A synonym for "frog" is _____.

Sample synonyms: croaker, amphibian, hopper

4. **SUMMARY**—When you summarize a story, you want to keep only the most important ideas. The rest of the writing can be done away with.

A. Read *The Frog and the Ox* again. Decide which event in the story is the most important for communicating the moral. This event is the action in the story that accompanies the main idea. In most fables, the moral of the story is the main idea but it appears first as part of the action of the story. Once you have decided what the main idea of the story is, circle or highlight it.

B. Underline any words that are essential to telling the story. Use these words to tell the story briefly in your summary.

C. Cross out any words or sentences that are extra details. These details might make the fable more fun to read, but they aren't necessary for readers to understand the main idea.

D. Summarize the fable in four sentences or less. You should feel free to rearrange words or add words as needed.

The Frog and the Ox
—Aesop's Fables

"Oh, Father," said a little Frog to the big one ~~sitting by the side of a pool,~~ "I have seen such a terrible monster! ~~It was as big as a mountain, with horns on its head, and a long tail, and it had hoofs divided in two.~~"

~~"Tush, tush, tush,"~~ said the old Frog, "that was only the Farmer's Ox. ~~It isn't so big either. He may be a little bit taller than I, but~~ I could easily make myself as broad. ~~Just you see!" So he blew himself out, and blew himself out, and blew himself out. "Was he as big as that?" asked the old Frog.~~

~~"Oh, much bigger than that," said the young Frog.~~

~~Again the old one blew himself out, and asked the young one if the Ox was as big as that.~~

~~"Bigger, Father, bigger," was the reply.~~

So the Frog took a deep breath, and blew ~~and blew and blew,~~ and swelled and ~~swelled and swelled. And then he said: "I'm sure the Ox is not as big as—"~~ But at that moment the conceited old Frog burst.

MORAL: *Self-conceit may lead to self-destruction.*

Summary:

Sample summary: A little Frog said to his father that he had seen a terrible monster. The big Frog said that the monster was only the Farmer's Ox and bragged that he could make himself just as broad. So the big Frog took a deep breath and blew and swelled till he burst.

_____

_____

_____

_____

_____

_____

5. **AMPLIFICATION**—Take your summary of *The Frog and the Ox* and make it longer.

- You can add description and details. What do the frogs look like? What sort of pool are the frogs sitting beside? What are some new ways in which the little Frog can describe the monstrous Ox? What does the old Frog look like as he is blowing himself up?

- You can add talking, which is called **dialogue**. Amplify the old Frog's boast, making it longer and even more conceited. What does the little Frog say as he sees his father swelling bigger and bigger? Does the Ox make any comment as he watches the old Frog blow up?

- You can expand the moral lesson by telling why "self-conceit may lead to self-destruction" and why it is important not to boast.

> Sample amplification:
>
> A little green Frog said to his big bullfrog father that he had seen a terrible monster. "It was as big as a house, and its thick skin was covered with long, shaggy hair. It almost crushed me as I was sitting in a puddle by the side of the road."
>
> Now the big Frog liked to show off for his son and he was a bit of a braggart as well. He laughed at the little Frog and said, "That monster is only the Farmer's Ox. And it's not as big as you think. Why, I can make myself just as big any day I choose. In fact, I can make myself even bigger than that runty creature." To prove his point, the big Frog started huffing and puffing, and he huffed and puffed till he looked like a green helium balloon.
>
> But the little Frog said to his pop, "You're not nearly as big as the Ox." So the big Frog huffed and puffed some more until he blew up with a loud bang! Even the Ox heard the noise and wondered if the Farmer had slammed the kitchen door.

_____

_____

_____

_____

_____

_____

_____

_____

_____

_____

_____

_____

_____

_____

_____

6. **WRITE YOUR OWN FABLE**—Write a short narrative using the same moral as that of *The Frog and the Ox*: "Self-conceit may lead to self-destruction." Use one set of the following animals or use your own.

- a little snake, a big snake, and a giraffe
- a little egret, a big egret, and a hippopotamus
- a little blowfish, a big blowfish, and a whale
- a little chick, a big hen, and an eagle

_____

_____

_____

_____

Stories will vary.

Sample fable:

Once there was a big mother hen and her little chick. The mother tried hard to teach her chick to be safe and protect himself. She knew the times when the eagle fed—usually in early morning and at dusk—and she told her chick to stay in the coop during those two hours of the day so that he couldn't be spied by the hungry eagle. The chick usually followed his mother's advice, but after proving himself strong in a contest among the other chicks, he boasted to his friends, "I have grown strong and smart and am not afraid of the eagle that feeds in the morning and at dusk. Today I will search for worms in the early morning." The other chicks were terrified and begged their friend not to do it. But the chick believed himself strong enough and watchful enough. In the early morning he left the coop to look for the juicy worm he could already taste. While he searched he did not notice the huge shadow of the eagle that flew across the sky just behind him. The chick's friends watching from the coop screeched at the top of their lungs, causing their friend to look up and see the shadow just as he came to a bush. He raced under the bush and escaped the eagle. If it hadn't been for his friends, he would have been eaten. MORAL: Self-conceit may lead to self-destruction.

_____

_____

_____

_____

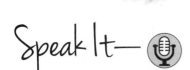

_____

_____

_____

_____

Speak It— 🎤

The following are two narrative poems about pride and conceit. Your teacher may ask you to memorize a stanza or a whole poem. Notice how the first poem is nearly the same as our fable *The Frog and the Ox*.

Lesson 3: Fable Refresher

The Frogs and the Bull

—from *Aesop, in Rhyme* by Marmaduke Park

A Bull once treading near a bog,
Displaced the **entrails** of a frog,
Who near his foot did trust them;
In fact, so great was the **contusion**,
And made of his inwards such confusion,
No art could re-adjust them.

It chanced that some who saw his fate,
Did to a friend the deed relate,
With croakings, groans, and hisses;
"The beast," said they, "in size excell'd
All other beasts." Their neighbor swell'd,
And ask'd, "as large as this is!"

"Oh, larger far than that," said they,
"Do not attempt it, madam, pray;"
But still the frog distended,
And said, "I'll burst, but I'll exceed,"
She tried, and burst herself indeed!
And so the matter ended.

MORAL:

Should you with pride inflate and swell,
As did the frog: then who can tell!
Your sides may crack, as has been shown,
And we with laughing crack our own.

This next poem was written by Heinrich Hoffmann, a psychiatrist and very popular writer of moral poems for children. "Phoebe Ann" first appeared in the book *Slovenly Betsy*. Instead of popping like a balloon, Phoebe experiences something equally shocking.

Phoebe Ann, the Proud Girl

—from *Slovenly Betsy* by Heinrich Hoffmann

This Phoebe Ann was a very proud girl,

Her nose had always an upward curl.

She thought herself better than all others beside,

And beat even the peacock himself in pride.

She thought the earth was so dirty and brown,

That never, by chance, would she look down;

And she held up her head in the air so high

That her neck began stretching by and by.

It stretched and it stretched; and it grew so long

That her parents thought something must be wrong

It stretched and stretched, and they soon began

To look up with fear at their Phoebe Ann.

They prayed her to stop her upward gaze,

But Phoebe kept on in her old proud ways,

Until her neck had grown so long and spare

That her head was more than her neck could bear—

And it bent to the ground, like a willow tree,

And brought down the head of this proud Phoebe,

Until whenever she went out a walk to take,

The boys would shout, "Here comes a snake!"

Her head got to be so heavy to drag on,

That she had to put it on a little wagon.

So don't, my friends, hold your head too high,

Or your neck may stretch, too, by and by.

Lesson 3: Fable Refresher

Lesson 3: Fable Refresher

Talk About It—

1. Answers will vary. Some people boast because they feel they aren't getting enough attention or they want to look better than other people. Or they may want to impress someone or make themselves feel important.

2. bragging

3. Like all boasters, Caesar was trying to tell people how great he was. In this case, Caesar was bragging about how easy it was for him to defeat the kingdom of Pontus. Unlike the frog, who blew up, Caesar actually lived up to his bragging words. The frog's bragging was empty.

4. When someone praises herself, most people can't stand to listen. When someone praises another person, it is much easier to believe and is much more acceptable. So Proverbs 27:2 is very wise advice.

Notes

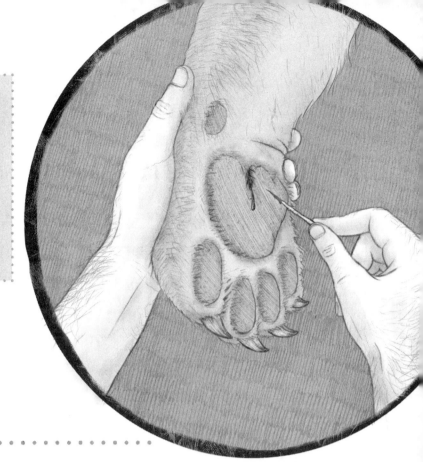

The purpose of this lesson is to introduce the idea of an outline as the skeleton of a story. In this lesson, your students will practice:

- outlining significant stories from Roman times

Please note that the three Roman stories in this lesson do not have to be outlined all at once. Feel free to return to this chapter for more practice. Outlining exercises can also be found in subsequent lessons.

Lesson 4 · · · · · · · · · · · · · · · · ·

Outlining a Narrative

Do skeletons make you nervous? If you're in school right now, chances are the room is full of skeletons. Of course, it helps that they are hidden inside a delightful mantle of flesh and skin. Be grateful for your skeleton! If you didn't have one, you would be a bouncy puddle of skin and organs on the floor, scooting around like a jellyfish or a slug.

Just as all people need a skeleton, narratives need a skeleton too. The skeleton of a story is called an **outline**. The outline of a story tells us what comes in the beginning, the middle, and the end. Not only that, the outline also tells us what parts are most important and what parts are less important. The most important parts of an outline are labeled with a Roman numeral (*I, II, III, IV* . . .). The next important parts are labeled with capital letters (*A, B, C, D* . . .), followed by standard numbers (*1, 2, 3, 4* . . .) and lowercase letters (*a, b, c, d* . . .).

To demonstrate this concept, let's start with a popular folk tale from England, *The Three Little Pigs.*

The Three Little Pigs

—adapted from *English Fairy Tales* by Joseph Jacobs

There was an old sow with three little pigs, and as she had not enough to keep them, she sent them out to seek their fortune. The first that went off met a man with a bundle of straw and said to him, "Please, man, give me that straw to build me a house."

The man gave him the straw, and the little pig built a house with it. Presently, along came a wolf, who knocked at the door and said, "Little pig, little pig, let me come in."

The pig answered, "Not by the hair of my chinny-chin-chin."

The wolf answered, "Then I'll huff and I'll puff, and I'll blow your house in."

So he huffed and he puffed, and he blew his house in and ate up the little pig.

The second little pig met a man with a bundle of sticks and said, "Please, man, give me those sticks to build a house."

The man gave him the sticks, and the pig built his house. Then along came the wolf, who said, "Little pig, little pig, let me come in."

"Not by the hair of my chinny-chin-chin."

"Then I'll puff and I'll huff, and I'll blow your house in."

So the wolf huffed and he puffed, and he puffed and he huffed. At last he blew the house down, and he ate up the little pig.

The third little pig met a man with a load of bricks and said, "Please, man, give me those bricks to build a house with."

So the man gave him the bricks, and he built his house with them. The wolf came, as he did to the other little pigs, and said, "Little pig, little pig, let me come in."

"Not by the hair of my chinny-chin-chin."

"Then I'll huff and I'll puff, and I'll blow your house in."

Well, he huffed and he puffed, and he puffed and he huffed, and he huffed and puffed, but he could *not* get the house down. When he found that he could not, with all his huffing and puffing, blow the house down, the wolf was very angry indeed. He declared that he *would* eat up the little pig and that he would go down the chimney after him.

Lesson 4: *Outlining a Narrative*

When the little pig saw what the wolf was about, he made up a blazing fire in the fireplace and hung a pot full of water over the fire. Just as the wolf was coming down the chimney, the pig took off the pot's cover, and in fell the wolf. The little pig put the cover on the pot in an instant, boiled up the wolf, and ate him for supper. The pig lived happily ever afterward.

The following is an outline based on the story of *The Three Little Pigs*:

I. Mother (sow) pig can't keep her piggy children.

    A. She sends them into the world.

    B. "Make your fortune," she tells them.

II. First pig and the house of straw

    A. The first pig meets a man who gives him some straw.

    B. The pig builds a straw house.

    C. The wolf says, "I'll huff and I'll puff, and I'll blow your house in."

    D. The wolf blows down the house and eats the pig.

III. Second pig and the house of sticks

    A. The second pig meets a man who gives him some sticks.

    B. The pig builds a stick house.

    C. The wolf says, "I'll huff and I'll puff, and I'll blow your house in."

    D. The wolf blows down the house and eats the pig.

IV. Third pig and the house of bricks

    A. The third pig meets a man who gives him some bricks.

    B. The pig builds a solid brick house.

    C. The wolf huffs and he puffs, and he puffs and he huffs, and he huffs and he puffs, but he can*not* blow the house down.

    D. The wolf says he will go down the chimney.

    E. The pig makes a blazing fire in the fireplace.

    F. The wolf goes down the chimney, where he lands in a boiling pot of water.

    G. The third pig eats the wolf for supper.

▶Why do you suppose an outline might be helpful to a writer?

Writers use outlines to help plan or plot their stories.

Imagine that you start out to write a long story without an outline. You write fifty pages and, somewhere in the middle, you realize that you are completely off track and you're not getting closer to the end. What's to be done? More than likely, you'll have to start writing all over again and forfeit some or all of the work you thought you had completed.

When a writer takes time to make an outline, he can see the entire story from beginning to end. He knows how to keep the middle focused and organized. He can spot any hole or missing piece in the story. He can keep the characters on track so that the ending is everything he wants it to be. The outline provides a plan that helps the author achieve his goal.

Writers and speakers often create outlines before they start writing even short stories or speeches. Just as you would look like mush without your skeleton, most writing projects lack sharpness without an outline.

At the end of this book you will outline and write your own story, but for now this information will help you to understand the plot of each story if you take time to outline it. Let's begin with three famous but fairly simple stories from old Rome.

The Fable of the Stomach

—adapted from The Story of the Romans by H.A. Guerber

The poor people of Rome, the **plebeians**, were tired of serving the rich **patricians**. They deserted the city and climbed into the surrounding hills, meaning never to return. By telling a persuasive fable, however, one patrician named Menenius induced the poor plebeians to come back. Here is the story he told:

All the different parts of the body once refused to work, saying that they were tired of serving the stomach.

The legs said, "What is the use of running about from morning till night, merely to find food enough to fill it?"

"We won't work for that lazy stomach either!" said the hands and arms. "Legs, if you'll keep still, we won't move either."

Lesson 4: *Outlining a Narrative*

"We are tired, too," said the teeth. "It is grind, grind, grind, all day long. The stomach can do its own work hereafter."

All the other parts of the body had some complaint to make about the stomach, and all agreed that they would not work any more to satisfy its wants. The legs ceased walking, the hands and arms stopped working, the teeth did not grind any more, and the empty stomach clamored in vain for its daily supply of food.

All the limbs were delighted at first with their rest, and when the empty stomach called for something to eat, they merely laughed. Their fun did not last very long, however, because the stomach, weak for want of food, soon ceased its cries. Then, after a while, the hands and arms and legs grew so weak that they could not move. Eventually the entire body fell down and died because the stomach, without food, could no longer supply it with strength to live.

The following is an outline of the most important events in this fable. Fill in the blank spaces with the correct information from the fable. For Roman numeral III you will need to supply the whole sentence.

 I. The body parts refuse to work.

  A. The legs quit.

  B. The _____ hands and arms _____ quit.

  C. The _____ teeth _____ quit.
 II. The body parts rest.

  A. The empty stomach _____ clamored in vain for food _____.

  B. The hands, arms, and legs _____ laughed at first, then grew weak _____.

 III. _____ The body fell down and died. _____

Androclus and the Lion

—from *Fifty Famous Stories Retold* by James Baldwin

This story is a detailed retelling of *The Mouse and the Lion* from *Aesop's Fables*. There is testimony by a Roman teacher that these events actually happened.

In Rome there was once a poor slave whose name was Androclus. His master was a cruel man, and so unkind to him that at last Androclus ran away.

He hid himself in a wild wood for many days; but there was no food to be found, and he grew so weak and sick that he thought he should die. So one day he crept into a cave and lay down, and soon he was fast asleep.

After awhile a great noise woke him up. A lion had come into the cave and was roaring loudly. Androclus was very much afraid, for he felt sure that the beast would kill him. Soon, however, he saw that the lion was not angry, but that he limped as though his foot hurt him.

Then Androclus grew so bold that he took hold of the lion's lame paw to see what was the matter. The lion stood quite still, and rubbed his head against the man's shoulder. He seemed to say, —

"I know that you will help me."

Androclus lifted the paw from the ground, and saw that it was a long, sharp thorn which hurt the lion so much. He took the end of the thorn in his fingers; then he gave a strong, quick pull, and out it came. The lion was full of joy. He jumped about like a dog, and licked the hands and feet of his new friend.

Androclus was not at all afraid after this; and when night came, he and the lion lay down and slept side by side.

For a long time, the lion brought food to Androclus every day; and the two became such good friends, that Androclus found his new life a very happy one.

One day some soldiers who were passing through the wood found Androclus in the cave. They knew who he was, and so took him back to Rome.

It was the law at that time that every slave who ran away from his master should be made to fight a hungry lion. So a fierce lion was shut up for a while without food, and a time was set for the fight.

Lesson 4: *Outlining a Narrative*

When the day came, thousands of people crowded to see the sport. They went to such places at that time very much as people now-a-days go to see a circus show or a game of baseball.

The door opened, and poor Androclus was brought in. He was almost dead with fear, for the roars of the lion could already be heard. He looked up, and saw that there was no pity in the thousands of faces around him.

Then the hungry lion rushed in. With a single bound he reached the poor slave. Androclus gave a great cry, not of fear, but of gladness. It was his old friend, the lion of the cave.

The people, who had expected to see the man killed by the lion, were filled with wonder. They saw Androclus put his arms around the lion's neck; they saw the lion lie down at his feet, and lick them lovingly; they saw the great beast rub his head against the slave's face as though he wanted to be petted. They could not understand what it all meant.

After a while they asked Androclus to tell them about it. So he stood up before them, and, with his arm around the lion's neck, told how he and the beast had lived together in the cave.

"I am a man," he said, "but no man has ever befriended me. This poor lion alone has been kind to me; and we love each other as brothers."

The people were not so bad that they could be cruel to the poor slave now. "Live and be free!" they cried. "Live and be free!"

Others cried, "Let the lion go free too! Give both of them their liberty!"

And so Androclus was set free, and the lion was given to him for his own. And they lived together in Rome for many years.

In the space provided, write down events that go with each main point listed:

I. Androclus escapes a cruel slave master and hides in the wild wood.

A. Sample answer: Starving, Androclus crawls into a cave to die. _____

_____

B. Sample answer: A lion enters the cave roaring loudly. _____

_____

II. Androclus and the lion become friends.

A. Sample answer: Androclus pulls a thorn from the lion's paw. _____

_____

B. Sample answer: The lion was grateful and became Androclus's friend. _____

_____

C. Sample answer: Like a faithful dog, the lion brings Androclus food to eat. _____

_____

III. Androclus is taken to Rome for punishment.

A. Sample answer: Some soldiers discover Androclus. _____

_____

B. Sample answer: Androclus must fight a hungry lion in the circus. _____

_____

C. Sample answer: The lion rushes out with a roar; the crowd expects it to kill Androclus. _

_____

1. Sample answer: The lion sent into the arena is the same lion Androclus met in the cave.

_____

2. Sample answer: Instead of killing Androclus, the lion lies down at his feet and licks him.

_____

IV. Androclus is set free.

A. Sample answer: Androclus is given the lion. _____

_____

B. Sample answer: The two friends live happily together in Rome. _____

_____

Cornelia's Jewels

—from *Fifty Famous Stories Retold* by James Baldwin

It was a bright morning in the old city of Rome many hundred years ago. In a vine-covered summer-house in a beautiful garden, two boys were standing. They were looking at their mother and her friend, who were walking among the flowers and trees.

"Did you ever see so handsome a lady as our mother's friend?" asked the younger boy, holding his tall brother's hand. "She looks like a queen."

"Yet she is not so beautiful as our mother," said the elder boy. "She has a fine dress, it is true; but her face is not noble and kind. It is our mother who is like a queen."

"That is true," said the other. "There is no woman in Rome so much like a queen as our own dear mother."

Soon Cornelia, their mother, came down the walk to speak with them. She was simply dressed in a plain white robe. Her arms and feet were bare, as was the custom in those days; and no rings nor chains glittered about her hands and neck. For her only crown, long braids of soft brown hair were coiled about her head; and a tender smile lit up her noble face as she looked into her sons' proud eyes.

"Boys," she said, "I have something to tell you."

They bowed before her, as Roman lads were taught to do, and said, "What is it, mother?"

"You are to dine with us to-day, here in the garden; and then our friend is going to show us that wonderful casket of jewels of which you have heard so much."

The brothers looked shyly at their mother's friend. Was it possible that she had still other rings besides those on her fingers? Could she have other gems besides those which sparkled in the chains about her neck?

When the simple outdoor meal was over, a servant brought the casket from the house. The lady opened it. Ah, how those jewels dazzled the eyes of the wondering boys! There were ropes of pearls, white as milk, and smooth as satin; heaps of shining rubies, red as the glowing coals; sapphires as blue as the sky that summer day; and diamonds that flashed and sparkled like the sunlight.

The brothers looked long at the gems.

"Ah!" whispered the younger; "if our mother could only have such beautiful things!"

At last, however, the casket was closed and carried carefully away.

"Is it true, Cornelia, that you have no jewels?" asked her friend. "Is it true, as I have heard it whispered, that you are poor?"

▲ *Cornelia, Mother of the Gracchi*
by Angelica Kauffman

"No, I am not poor," answered Cornelia, and as she spoke she drew her two boys to her side; "for here are my jewels. They are worth more than all your gems."

I am sure that the boys never forgot their mother's pride and love and care; and in after years, when they had become great men in Rome, they often thought of this scene in the garden. And the world still likes to hear the story of Cornelia's jewels.

Create an outline for the story *Cornelia's Jewels* using Roman numerals (*I, II, III*) for the most important events and capital letters (*A, B, C*) for less important events or quotations that are related. Use standard numbers (*1, 2, 3*) for minor points. Ask yourself, "What are the natural parts of the story and how can they be divided up?"

Lesson 4: Outlining a Narrative

Sample outline:

I. Cornelia is visited by a Roman noblewoman.

    A. The visitor wears a fine dress.

    B. Cornelia's two boys think their mother looks more beautiful than the visitor.

II. Cornelia and the noblewoman share an outdoor meal.

    A. Cornelia invites her sons to dine with them.

    B. The visitor shows off her casket of jewels.

    C. The jewels dazzle the boys' eyes.

III. Cornelia is called poor by the visitor.

IV. Cornelia shows off her two sons.

    A. "These are my gems."

    B. The boys never forget their mother's pride.

The purpose of this lesson is to introduce the hook as a way to grab an audience's attention and to discuss the importance of beginning a story well.
In this lesson, your students will practice:

- outlining
- dictionary skills
- finding synonyms for nouns, adjectives, and verbs
- summarizing a myth
- creating story hooks with description and dialogue
- elocution

Lesson 5 ··

Story Beginnings

In the previous book in this series, *Writing & Rhetoric: Narrative I*, we discussed how the beginning and end of a story are somewhat easier to write than the middle. Once you have a beginning idea, you can usually see the ending somewhere off in the distance, just as, if you stand on the edge of a wide lake, you can most likely see the opposite shore.

The harder part is how to get from one shore to the other. If you swim, you'll need to use different strokes and pace yourself. If you row a boat, you'll have to be careful not to run into submerged objects. Will the weather turn stormy and cause the waves to chop? Will you meet an island in the middle or a great, leaping fish? Both sides of the lake, the beginning and end of the journey, are solid ground. It's the middle that's full of mystery. In the same way, most writers begin their stories with the end in mind. It's the middle that takes most of the work, because you never know what challenges you might encounter as you move from beginning to end.

Let's put off the middle until the next lesson. For now, let's have some practice with story beginnings.

The first task of a writer or speaker is to grab the attention of her audience. If she doesn't succeed in grabbing attention right from the start, her audience may nod off and then her wonderful middle and end will be all for nothing. The attention grabber of a story is known as the **hook**. Take a look at some selections from some well-known novels for children that begin with famous hooks:

- There was a boy called Eustace Scrubb, and he almost deserved it. His parents called him Eustace Clarence and masters called him Scrubb. I can't tell you how his friends spoke to him because he had none. —from *The Voyage of the Dawn Treader* by C.S. Lewis

- "Where's Papa going with that ax?" said Fern to her mother as they were setting the table for breakfast. "Out to the hoghouse," replied Mrs. Arable. "Some pigs were born last night." —from *Charlotte's Web* by E.B. White

- Way out at the edge of a tiny little town was an old overgrown garden, and in the garden was an old house, and in the house lived Pippi Longstocking. She was nine years old, and she lived there all alone. She had no father or mother and that was of course very nice because there was no one to tell her to go to bed. —from *Pippi Longstocking* by Astrid Lindgren

- "Tom!" No answer. "Tom!" No answer. "What's gone with that boy, I wonder? You, Tom!" No answer. —from *The Adventures of Tom Sawyer* by Mark Twain

Getting a story started can be a difficult task for some people. Sometimes you can't think of a single idea. That old, blank piece of paper stares back at you like a lazy cat, never blinking its eyes. You just want to wad up the paper and throw it at the wall. Reading and imitation can help you with story beginnings. To practice this, read *The Fifth Labor of Hercules*, and while you read, be thinking of another way to begin the story.

The Fifth Labor of Hercules

—from *Gods and Heroes* by R.E. Francillon

The next labor which Eurystheus laid upon Hercules was to clean out a stable. That does not sound [like] very much after the others. But then the stable was that of Augeas, King of Elis, which was at once the largest and the dirtiest in the whole world.

Augeas had a **prodigious** number of oxen and goats, and the stable in which they were all kept had never been cleaned. The result was a mountain of filth and litter, which not even Hercules could clear away in a lifetime—not, of course, from want of strength, but from want of time. Hercules beheld with disgust and dismay the loathsome and **degrading toil** in which he was to spend the rest of his days. The other labors had at least been honorable, and befitting a prince: this would have appalled a scavenger.

"It is very good of such a hero as you," said Augeas, "to undertake to clean my stable. It really does want cleaning, as you see: and it was very kind of Eurystheus to think of it. You shall not find me ungrateful. I will give you one ox and one goat in every ten—when the job is done."

Lesson 5: *Story Beginnings*

He could very safely promise this, because he knew that the job could never be done.

"I am not serving for hire," said Hercules. "Nevertheless it is only right that you should not let your stable get into such a state as this, and then get it put right for nothing. You want a lesson: and you shall have it, too."

Seeing that his strength would be wasted in such toil, Hercules went to work with his brain as well. Through the land of Elis ran the river Alpheus. Hercules carefully studied the country; and having laid his plans, he dug a channel from near the source of the river to one of the entrances of the stable. Then, damming up the old channel, he let the stream run into the new. The new course was purposely made narrow, so that the current might be exceedingly strong.

When all was ready, he opened the sluice at one entrance of the stable, so that the water poured in a flood through the whole building, and out at a gate on the other side. And it had all been so managed that when the river had poured through, and was shut off again, all the filth and litter had been carried away by the Alpheus underground, and the stable had been washed clean, without a scrap of refuse to be found anywhere. For the Alpheus you must know, did not run into the sea, like other rivers. It disappeared down a deep chasm, then ran through a natural tunnel under the sea, and rose again, far away, in the island of Sicily, where it had brought to Ceres the news from underground. Thus everything thrown into it in Elis came up again in Sicily—and the Sicilians must have been considerably astonished at that extraordinary eruption of stable litter. Perhaps it is that which, acting as manure, has helped to make Sicily so fertile.

Hercules made a point of claiming his price. But Augeas said:

"Nonsense! A bargain is a bargain. You undertook to clean my stable: and you have done nothing of the kind. No work, no pay."

"What can you mean?" asked Hercules. "Surely I have cleaned your stable—you will not find in it a broken straw."

"No," said Augeas. "It was the Alpheus did that: not you."

"But it was I who used the Alpheus—"

"Yes; no doubt. But the impudence of expecting me to pay a tenth of all my flocks and herds for an idea so simple that I should have thought of it myself, if you hadn't, just by chance, happened to think of it before me! You have not earned your wages. You cleaned the stable by an unfair trick: and it was the river cleaned it—not you."

"Very well," said Hercules grimly. "If you had paid me honestly, I would have given you your goats and your oxen back again; for, as I told you, I do not serve for reward. But now I perceive that I have not quite cleaned your stable. There is still one piece of dirt left in it—and that is a cheating knave, Augeas by name. So, as I cannot go back to Mycenæ till my work is done—"

He was about to throw Augeas into the river, to follow the rest of the litter: and about what afterwards happened, different people tell different things. I very strongly agree, however, with those who tell that Hercules spared the life of Augeas after having given him a lesson: for certainly he was not worth the killing. And I am the more sure of this because, after his death, Augeas was honored as hero—which surely would not have happened if he had not learned to keep both his stables and his promises clean before he died.

Tell It Back—Narration 🅐

1. **ORAL NARRATION**: Without looking at the text, tell the myth of *The Fifth Labor of Hercules* as best as you remember it using your own words. Try not to leave out any important details.

Here are the first three sentences to help you get started:

The next labor which Eurystheus laid upon Hercules was to clean out a stable. That does not sound [like] very much after the others. But then the stable was that of Augeas, King of Elis, which was at once the largest and the dirtiest in the whole world.

Lesson 5: *Story Beginnings*

2. **OUTLINE**: Create an outline for *The Fifth Labor of Hercules* using Roman numerals (*I, II, III*) for the most important events and capital letters (*A, B, C*) for less important events. Use standard numbers (*1, 2, 3*) for minor points.

Sample outline:
    I. Eurystheus orders Hercules to clean the stables of King Augeas.
      A. They are the largest and dirtiest in the world.
      B. There is more filth than Hercules could clean in a lifetime.
    II. Augeas is pleased to have Hercules's help.
      A. He promises one-tenth of all of his livestock.
      B. The job must be finished before Hercules is paid.
    III. Hercules uses his brains.
      A. He dams up the Alpheus River.
      B. The dam sends the river through the stable.
      C. The stable filth ends up in Sicily.
    IV. Augeas takes back his promise.
      A. He claims the river cleaned the stable, not Hercules.
      B. Hercules is angered.
        1. He says there is "one piece of dirt left."
        2. He threatens to throw Augeas into the river.

Talk About It—

1. One of the biggest cleanup jobs in history was caused by the earthquake in Haiti, an island in the Caribbean Sea. Apart from terrible loss of life, nearly 300,000 buildings were reduced to rubble. Here's another way to look at it: The earthquake produced 20 million cubic meters of mess. Imagine having to clean that up! What is your attitude toward cleaning up? Are you a willing worker like Hercules or a lazy king like Augeas?

2. Look over the story beginnings in the introduction of this lesson. Tell how each one is good for grabbing attention.

3. Now that you have read several beginnings, judge the strength of the beginning of *The Fifth Labor of Hercules*.

4. Which is more interesting, the beginning of *The Fifth Labor of Hercules* or the end? Why?

5. Why do you suppose the attention grabber in a story is called the hook?

Go Deeper—

1. What kind of narrative do you think *The Fifth Labor of Hercules* is?
   a. parable
   b. myth
   c. fairy tale
   d. history

2. Which of these proverbs do you think best expresses the main idea of *The Fifth Labor of Hercules*?
   a. Hard work never did anybody any harm.
   b. It's no use locking the stable after the horse has run away.
   c. The remedy for dirt is soap and water.
   d. A clever person turns great troubles into little ones.

Lesson 5: Story Beginnings

3. Because the stables of Augeas are filled with a mountain of manure, a "prodigious number" of oxen and goats probably means:

    a. a small number

    b. a disgusting number

    c. a huge number

    d. a smelly number

4. The adjective "degrading" comes from the combined Latin words *des* (down) and *gradus* (step). With the Latin in mind, what word most closely matches the meaning of "degrading"? ("Hercules beheld with disgust and dismay the loathsome and degrading toil.")

    a. disgraceful

    b. easy

    c. falling

    d. laughable

5. Hercules beheld with disgust and dismay the loathsome and degrading toil in which he was to spend the rest of his days. Write your own complete sentence defining the word "toil."

    ___ Sample sentence: Toil is hard work. _____

    _____

    _____

    _____

6. Now look up the word "toil" in a dictionary and write it down. Is your definition similar to the dictionary definition?

    ___ Toil is long, difficult, and tiring labor. _____

    _____

    _____

    _____

7. Use a thesaurus to find synonyms for the word "toil." Use a synonym for "toil" in your own sentence. Make sure your sentence helps the reader to understand the word's meaning.

> Sample synonyms for "toil": hard work, labor, drudgery
> Sample sentence: Cleaning up after the party was such drudgery that Meg felt like Cinderella.

_____

_____

Writing Time—

1. **DICTATION**—Your teacher will read a little part of *The Fifth Labor of Hercules* back to you. Please listen carefully! After your teacher reads once, she will read slowly again and include the punctuation marks. Your task will be to write down the sentences as your teacher reads them one by one.

> Modify according to student level. Please note that this is the first time you use quotation marks in a dictation. Be sure to help the students understand where to place this punctuation properly.
>
> Seeing that his strength would be wasted in such toil, Hercules went to work with his brain as well.
>
> "What can you mean?" asked Hercules. "Surely I have cleaned your stable."

_____

2. **SENTENCE PLAY**—<u>The stable was at once the largest and the dirtiest in the whole world.</u>

The words "at once" tell us that the stable is two things at the same time: largest and dirtiest. Find two words that describe each of the nouns in the following similar sentences.

a. The woman's hair was at once _____

> Sample sentence: The woman's hair was at once the longest and the stringiest in the whole world.

_____

_____.

b. The playground slide was at once _____

> ____ Sample sentence: The playground slide was at once the tallest and the fastest in the whole world.

_____.

c. Now make up your own sentence following the same pattern.

> ____ Sample sentence: The gorilla was at once the hairiest and the ugliest in the whole world.

_____

_____

3. **COPIOUSNESS**—In writing copiously for this lesson, you are going to replace nouns and adjectives with synonyms. You will also replace verbs with verb synonyms.

A. Mark the nouns (there are three) and the verbs (there are two) in the following sentence. Place an *N* over the nouns and a *V* over the verbs.

- Remember that a noun is a person, place, thing, or idea. Examples: police officer, park, slide, fun
- The name "Hercules" is a special type of noun called a proper noun. A **proper noun** names a specific person, place, thing, or idea. Examples: Henrietta, Spain, Kleenex
- A verb is often the action word of the sentence. Examples: run, slide, kick, dance, fly, fall, bump, laugh, cry

       N   V

Seeing that his <u>strength</u> would be <u>wasted</u> in such

N   V   N

<u>toil</u>, Hercules <u>went to work</u> with his <u>brain</u> as well.

B. Use synonyms to replace the underlined words in the sentence you labeled and rewrite the sentence.

> ___ Sample sentence: Seeing that his might would be lost in such work, Hercules started to labor with his mind as well.

_____

_____

C. Rewrite the sentence so that it carries the same meaning, but start with the word "Hercules."

Sample sentence: Hercules saw that his strength would be wasted in such toil and went to work with his brain as well.

_____

_____

_____

D. Rewrite the sentence so that it carries the same meaning, but start with the words "with his brain."

Sample sentence: With his brain, Hercules went to work, seeing that his strength would be wasted in such toil.

_____

_____

_____

E. Mark the verbs in the following sentence with a *V* and find synonyms for them. Rewrite the sentence two times using different verbs. Use a thesaurus only if you get stuck.

V   V
She cried and laughed at the same time.

i. Sample sentence: She wept and giggled at the same time. _____

_____

_____

ii. Sample sentence: She sobbed and snickered at the same time. _____

_____

_____

_____

Lesson 5: Story Beginnings

4. **SUMMARY**—Just as you learn about the skeleton of a story by constructing an outline, you can learn about the most important ideas of a story by writing a summary. If you think of the story as a barrel of grapes, writing a summary is like crushing the grapes to get only the juice. When you summarize a story, you want to keep only the most important ideas. The rest of the writing can be done away with.

A. Read *The Fifth Labor of Hercules* again. Decide which idea is the main idea and circle or highlight it.

B. Underline any words essential to telling the story. Use these words to tell the story briefly in your summary.

C. This time you won't cross out any words or sentences that are extra details. In your mind, try to get rid of any words that simply make the story more fun to read but aren't necessary to the main idea.**A**

D. Rewrite the story in five sentences or less.

> **A** The idea here is for students to create summaries without depending on crossing out words on paper as they did in the previous two books. Oral narration is a great way to practice summary.
>
> Challenge students to narrate the entire story with a minimum of sentences.

The Fifth Labor of Hercules

—from *Gods and Heroes* by R.E. Francillon

The next labor which Eurystheus laid upon Hercules was to clean out a stable. That does not sound [like] very much after the others. But then the stable was that of Augeas, King of Elis, which was at once the largest and the dirtiest in the whole world.

Augeas had a prodigious number of oxen and goats, and the stable in which they were all kept had never been cleaned. The result was a mountain of filth and litter, which not even Hercules could clear away in a lifetime—not, of course, from want of strength, but from want of time. Hercules beheld with disgust and dismay the loathsome and degrading toil in which he was to spend the rest of his days. The other labors had at least been honorable, and befitting a prince: this would have appalled a scavenger.

"It is very good of such a hero as you," said Augeas, "to undertake to clean my stable. It really does want cleaning, as you see: and it was very kind of Eurystheus to think of it. You shall not find me ungrateful. I will give you one ox and one goat in every ten—when the job is done."

He could very safely promise this, because he knew that the job could never be done.

"I am not serving for hire," said Hercules. "Nevertheless it is only right that you should not let your stable get into such a state as this, and then get it put right for nothing. You want a lesson: and you shall have it, too."

Seeing that his strength would be wasted in such toil, Hercules went to work with his brain as well. Through the land of Elis ran the river Alpheus. Hercules carefully studied the country; and having laid his plans, dug a channel from near the source of the river to one of the entrances of the stable. Then, damming up the old channel, he let the stream run into the new. The new course was purposely made narrow, so that the current might be exceedingly strong. When all was ready, he opened the sluice at one entrance of the stable, so that the water poured in a flood through the whole building, and out at a gate on the other side. And it had all been so managed that when the river had poured through, and was shut off again, all the filth and litter had been carried away by the Alpheus underground, and the stable had been washed clean, without a scrap of refuse to be found anywhere. For the Alpheus you must know, did not run into the sea, like other rivers. It disappeared down a deep chasm, then ran through a natural tunnel under the sea, and rose again, far away, in the island of Sicily, where it had brought to Ceres the news from underground. Thus everything thrown into it in Elis came up again in Sicily—and the Sicilians must have been considerably astonished at that extraordinary eruption of stable litter. Perhaps it is that which, acting as manure, has helped to make Sicily so fertile.

Hercules made a point of claiming his price. But Augeas said:

"Nonsense! A bargain is a bargain. You undertook to clean my stable: and you have done nothing of the kind. No work, no pay."

"What can you mean?" asked Hercules. "Surely I have cleaned your stable—you will not find in it a broken straw."

"No," said Augeas. "It was the Alpheus did that: not you."

"But it was I who used the Alpheus—"

"Yes; no doubt. But the impudence of expecting me to pay a tenth of all my flocks and herds for an idea so simple that I should have thought of it myself, if you hadn't, just by chance, happened to think of it before me! You have not earned your wages. <u>You cleaned the stable by an unfair trick: and it was the river cleaned it—not you.</u>"

"Very well," said Hercules grimly. "If you had paid me honestly, I would have given you your goats and your oxen back again; for, as I told you, I do not serve for reward. But now I perceive that I have not quite cleaned your stable. There is still one piece of dirt left in it—and that is <u>a cheating knave, Augeas by name</u>. So, as I cannot go back to Mycenæ till my work is done—"

He was <u>about to throw Augeas into the river</u>, to follow the rest of the litter: and about what afterwards happened, different people tell different things. I very strongly agree, however, with those who tell that Hercules spared the life of Augeas after having given him a lesson: for certainly he was not worth the killing. And I am the more sure of this because, after his death, Augeas was honored as hero—which surely would not have happened if he had not learned to keep both his stables and his promises clean before he died.

Summary:

___ Sample summary: Hercules was sent to Elis to clean out the filthiest stable in the world,
    which belonged to King Augeas. Using his brain as well as his strength, Hercules diverted the
___ River Alpheus through the stable. The river washed out all the filth and litter, and Hercules
    claimed his prize—a tenth of Augeas's herd. When Augeas refused to pay, Hercules threat-
___ ened to throw him in the river.

_____

_____

_____

_____

_____

_____

5. **STORY HOOKS**—Here again is the beginning of *The Fifth Labor of Hercules*:

The next labor which Eurystheus laid upon Hercules was to clean out a stable. That does not sound [like] very much after the others. But then the stable was that of Augeas, King of Elis, which was at once the largest and the dirtiest in the whole world.

As far as hooks go, it's not too bad. We are immediately interested in a story in which the strongest man in the world must clean out the dirtiest stable in the world. Despite its being a pretty good beginning, let's try to make it even better. Allow your students to pick two of the three exercises to complete.

A. Description of Hercules: Obviously, the main character of the story is Hercules. In Greek and Roman mythology he was a demigod, or a half-god, the son of Jupiter (Zeus) and Alcmene, a princess of Mycenæ. Hercules was famous for his enormous strength and for using a lion skin to cover his nakedness. Make up a beginning to the story that includes a description of Hercules. Feel free to use the bust of Commodus as *Hercules* or Antonio del Pollaiuolo's painting of *Hercules and the Hydra* as a starting place. Your story beginning should grab your reader's attention by using descriptive words.

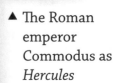

_____

_____

_____

▲ The Roman emperor Commodus as *Hercules*

◀ Antonio del Pollaiuolo's *Hercules and the Hydra*

_____

_____

_____

Lesson 5: *Story Beginnings*

Sample description: Hercules strode into the room half naked and garbed with a lion skin around his waist and back. The lion's head, with its massive mouth, came up around his head like a hood and covered his curly locks. And what curly locks he had! They twined around his face and head in a riot of wispy strands like ivy or morning glory. First and foremost, King Eurystheus observed Hercules's terrifying muscles and felt very weak and puny.

_____

_____

_____

_____

_____

_____

B. **DIALOGUE**—King of Tiryns: Unless you know the whole story of *The Twelve Labors of Hercules*, you may not recognize the character Eurystheus. Eurystheus was ruler of a walled fort and city in Greece named Tiryns. He was also Hercules's bitterest enemy because he was jealous of his superhuman strength. With the help of the goddess Hera, he forced Hercules to perform twelve labors. In each case, Eurystheus hoped that Hercules would be killed. Write a new beginning to *The Fifth Labor of Hercules* by letting your reader know that Eurystheus is king of Tiryns, Hercules's enemy, and put words into his mouth as he orders Hercules to clean the Augean stable.

▲ *The Mask of Agamemnon*

Sample dialogue: "You again!" spat Eurystheus. "So you didn't die in the last labor?" The king of Tiryns glowered for a moment, then forced himself to smile warmly. But the smile looked sinister. "I'm so glad you're still alive."

"Glad?" laughed Hercules. "I doubt it. Each labor has been worse than the last."

"No, seriously," Eurystheus laughed too. "I have a friend, a King Augeas of Elis, and he has a little stable that needs cleaning. You wouldn't mind cleaning a little stable would you?"

_____

_____

_____

_____

_____

_____

_____

_____

C. Description of the stable: As a hook, start out *The Fifth Labor of Hercules* with a description of the filthy Augean stables. Use as many of your senses as you can to describe the disgusting scene of oxen, goats, and manure. Describe the smell as well as the ugly sights and sounds. Describe Hercules's dismay when he first sets eyes on it.

> Sample description: Even before he saw the stable, Hercules almost fell down from the horrible stink that filled the air. It smelled like the rotting carcass of some enormous creature— a giant dead bird, maybe, or a giant fish. Waves of flies, like flocks of birds, darkened the sky and landed in swarms on anything alive, going down ears and up noses. Hercules staggered back when he saw the huge wooden building housing thousands of animals. It was bigger than the theatres in old Greece, and the manure was thigh deep.

_____

_____

_____

_____

_____

_____

_____

_____

Lesson 5: *Story Beginnings*

Speak It— 🎤

Play the "Um" Game: When someone speaks off the top of his head, he is making an impromptu or spontaneous speech. In this exercise, your teacher will give you a subject and you must talk continuously about it for one minute. You must tell your class everything you can think of on the subject. Here's the catch: You may not say, "ah," "um," or "like" for that entire minute. If you do, you lose your turn.

Here are some possible topics. The first set is related to this story. The second set is more general.

- cleaning up after a pet
- cleaning a stable
- building muscles
- the worst mess
- cheaters

- winter
- summer
- desserts
- animals
- amusement parks
- favorite book
- Thanksgiving
- pets
- Egyptians
- Hebrews
- Greeks
- Romans

Lesson 5: Story Beginnings

Talk About It—

1. Answers will vary. Ask students what sort of jobs they do around the house. Are they willing workers or do they give their parents a hard time? What sort of jobs do your students enjoy?

2. *The Voyage of the Dawn Treader*: A boy without friends is unusual, so the reader wants to know why he is friendless. The phrase "and he almost deserved it" creates curiosity because the reader will want to know why Eustace almost deserved his name. What is it about Eustace, or what has he done, that makes him deserve his name?

   Charlotte's Web: We know that the ax spells trouble for the pigs. At least one of the pigs is in danger.

   Pippi Longstocking: A nine-year-old who lives alone and who has no bedtime is immediately strange and interesting.

   Adventures of Tom Sawyer: Where is Tom? Someone is hollering for Tom, but he doesn't answer. Who is hollering, and why? The questions draw us in.

3. It is pretty strong. Hercules must clean up the largest stable in the world, a nasty job that none of us wants to do. That makes the story interesting from the start.

4. The beginning of the story is more interesting. It involves a great challenge and problem to solve, which makes us curious.

   The end is a little weak because we don't really know what happens to King Augeas. The ending would be stronger without the uncertainty. Perhaps if Hercules had thrown Augeas into the river we would find ourselves more interested.

5. Like the hook at the end of a fishing line, the attention grabber is supposed to "hook" the reader and cause her to keep reading.

Notes

_____

_____

_____

_____

_____

_____

_____

_____

_____

_____

_____

_____

_____

_____

_____

The purpose of this lesson is to introduce the concepts of the main character (protagonist), character traits, and simile.

In this lesson, your students will practice:

- critical thinking
- outlining
- building copiousness with synonyms
- changing dialogue
- changing point of view
- changing the protagonist

Teachers, please remember that you may not want to tackle changing dialogue, changing point of view, and changing the protagonist all in one lesson. These exercises are provided so that you have ample choice to decide what your class should practice.

Lesson 6

Main Character— The Protagonist

Once you've written the beginning of your story, you have set sail. You are now on your voyage toward a magnificent ending. If the beginning of the story is all about grabbing the reader's attention, what is the middle of the story all about? Well, of course, you want to hold on to the reader's attention once you've grabbed it. For this, interesting characters and conflict (which you'll learn about in the next lesson) are essential!

Storywriters must create characters that readers care about. Readers should especially care about the main character, who is often the hero of the story. Another word for the main character is **protagonist**. A protagonist was the lead actor in Greek drama, and we continue to use that term today to indicate the main character of a story.

Think of the main character, or protagonist, as a good friend. If your friend was in danger, you would never hang up the phone on him, would you? If your friend was celebrating a birthday, you would never turn out the lights and go home. By the same token, your readers will not drop your story if they like your main character.

What are some things that make a main character likeable? Think about the things that make people likeable to you. Do you have a favorite aunt or uncle? Do you have a favorite teacher or classmate? You probably like the special way that person smiles, talks, and laughs. You like the way that person gives you hugs or shakes your hand. You like that person's sense of adventure, or you trust the person's truthfulness. Or you may like that person because she is a bit strange—strange in a nice way!

One of the storybook characters I love best is Anne Shirley from *Anne of Green Gables*. She is definitely strange in a nice way. Her imagination is always flying away with her, and her tongue flies along with it. Here is Anne making an apology to a neighbor lady after screaming at her:

> "Oh, Mrs. Lynde, I am so extremely sorry," she said with a quiver in her voice. "I could never express all my sorrow, no, not if I used up a whole dictionary. You must just imagine it. I behaved terribly to you—and I've disgraced the dear friends, Matthew and Marilla, who have let me stay at Green Gables although I'm not a boy. I'm a dreadfully wicked and ungrateful girl, and I deserve to be punished and cast out by respectable people forever. It was very wicked of me to fly into a temper because you told me the truth. It WAS the truth; every word you said was true. My hair is red and I'm freckled and skinny and ugly. What I said to you was true, too, but I shouldn't have said it. Oh, Mrs. Lynde, please, please, forgive me. If you refuse it will be a lifelong sorrow on a poor little orphan girl, would you, even if she had a dreadful temper? Oh, I am sure you wouldn't. Please say you forgive me, Mrs. Lynde."

You might say that Anne is a drama queen. She has a way of adding comedy and tragedy to everything she says.

Most main characters, like all people, have something quirky or unusual about them. These **character traits** establish that the character is one of a kind and memorable to the reader. A trait is any feature that makes a person unique: height, weight, hair, eye color, and personality. It can be anything from a bad habit (biting fingernails, playing with gum) to a physical trait (thick glasses, a peg leg) to a manner of speaking ("Shiver me timbers!").

Another well-known book, *Winnie-the-Pooh*, is full of characters that have interesting traits. Winnie the Pooh describes himself as a "bear of very little brain," and we see that this is true when he risks his neck to steal honey from a bee's nest high in a tree. In fact, honey is the most prominent thought in Pooh's little brain. Even so, Pooh is a lovable character because he is kind and helpful to his friends. His manner of speaking is also quirky, for he is always saying, "Oh, bother!" and making up little ditties like "Rum-tum-tiddle-um-tum."

Let's take a look at another character, this one found in a tale from India. While you read, ask yourself what makes the Brahmin an interesting protagonist. What are his character traits?

Lesson 6: *Main Character—The Protagonist*

The Brahmin, the Tiger, and the Jackal

—adapted from *Stories to Tell to Children* by Sara Cone Bryant

Do you know what a Brahmin is? A Brahmin is a member of the Hindu priestly class, which includes poets, priests, and teachers.

One day in India, a Brahmin came walking down a dusty country road, his sandals clip-clopping under his feet. As he walked along, he hummed to himself and tugged thoughtfully at his long, white beard. Presently, the Brahmin came upon a Tiger shut up in a strong iron cage. The villagers had caught him and shut him up there for his wickedness.

"Oh, good Brahmin, kind Brahmin," said the Tiger, "please let me out to get a little drink! I am so thirsty, and there is no water here."

"But Brother Tiger," said the Brahmin, tugging at his beard, "you know if I should let you out, you would spring on me and eat me up."

"Never, dear Brahmin!" said the Tiger. "Never in the world would I do such an ungrateful thing! Never would I dream of double-crossing you! Just let me out a little minute, to get a little, little drink of water, sweet Brahmin!"

Now the Brahmin was a kind-hearted man and believed that the animals were his brothers. So he unlocked the door and let the Tiger out. The moment he was out, the **duplicitous** Tiger sprang on the Brahmin and was about to eat him up.

"But, Brother Tiger," said the Brahmin as his bony knees knocked together, "you promised you would not. It is not fair or just that you should eat me, when I set you free."

"It is perfectly right and just," said the Tiger, "and I shall eat you up."

However, the Brahmin argued so hard that at last the Tiger agreed to wait and ask the first five whom they should meet whether it was fair for him to eat the Brahmin and that he would abide by their decision.

The first thing they came to, to ask, was an old Banyan Tree by the wayside. (A banyan tree is a kind of fruit tree.)

"Brother Banyan," said the Brahmin eagerly, tugging at his beard, "does it seem to you right or just that this Tiger should eat me, when I set him free from his cage?"

The Banyan Tree looked down at them and spoke in a tired voice. "In the summer," he said, "when the sun is hot, men come and sit in the cool of my shade and refresh themselves with the fruit of my branches. But when evening falls and they are rested, they break my twigs and scatter my leaves and stone my boughs for more fruit. Men are an ungrateful race. Let the Tiger eat the Brahmin."

The Tiger sprang to eat the Brahmin, and the Brahmin's bony knees knocked together. The Brahmin said, "Wait, wait; we have asked only one. We have still four to ask."

Presently they came to a place where an old Bullock was lying by the road. The Brahmin went up to him and said, "Brother Bullock, oh, Brother Bullock, does it seem to you a fair thing that this Tiger should eat me up after I have just freed him from a cage?"

The Bullock looked up and answered in a deep, grumbling voice, "When I was young and strong my master used me hard, and I served him well. I carried heavy loads and carried them far. Now that I am old and weak and cannot work, he leaves me without food or water, to die by the wayside. Men are a thankless lot. Let the Tiger eat the Brahmin."

Lesson 6: *Main Character—The Protagonist*

The Tiger sprang, and the Brahmin's bony knees knocked together. He spoke very quickly: "Oh, but this is only the second, Brother Tiger; you promised to ask five."

The Tiger grumbled a good deal, but at last he went on again with the Brahmin. After a time they saw an Eagle high overhead. The Brahmin called up to him imploringly, "Oh, Brother Eagle, Brother Eagle! Tell us if it seems to you fair that this Tiger should eat me up, when I have just saved him from a frightful cage."

The Eagle soared slowly overhead a moment, then he came lower and spoke in a thin, clear voice. "I live high in the air," he said, "and I do no man any harm. Yet as often as they find my nest, men stone my young and rob my eggs and shoot at me with arrows. Men are a cruel breed. Let the Tiger eat the Brahmin!"

The Tiger sprang upon the Brahmin to eat him up, and this time the Brahmin's bony knees knocked together and his teeth chattered. He had very hard work to persuade the Tiger to wait. At last he did persuade him, however, and they walked on together. And in a little while they saw an old Alligator lying half buried in mud and slime at the river's edge.

"Brother Alligator, oh, Brother Alligator!" said the Brahmin. "Does it seem at all right or fair to you that this Tiger should eat me up, when I have just now let him out of a cage?"

The old Alligator turned in the mud and grunted and snorted. Then he said, "I lie here in the mud all day, as harmless as a pigeon. I hunt no man, yet every time a man sees me, he throws stones at me and pokes me with sharp sticks and jeers at me. Men are a worthless lot. Let the Tiger eat the Brahmin!"

At this the Tiger was bound to eat the Brahmin at once, and the Brahmin's whole body danced with fear. The poor man had to remind the Tiger, again and again, that they had asked only four.

"Wait till we've asked one more! Wait until we see a fifth!" he begged.

Finally, the Tiger walked on with him.

After a time, they met a little Jackal coming gaily down the road toward them.

"Oh, Brother Jackal, dear Brother Jackal," said the Brahmin, "give us your opinion! Do you think it right or fair that this Tiger should eat me, when I set him free from a terrible cage?"

"Beg pardon?" said the little Jackal.

"I said," said the Brahmin, raising his voice, "do you think it is fair that the Tiger should eat me, when I set him free from his cage?"

"Cage?" said the little Jackal vacantly.

"Yes, yes, his cage," said the Brahmin. "We want your opinion. Do you think—"

"Oh," said the little Jackal, "you want my opinion? Then may I beg you to speak a little more loudly and make the matter quite clear? I am a little slow of understanding. Now what was it?"

"Do you think," said the Brahmin, "it is right for this Tiger to eat me, when I set him free from his cage?"

"What cage?" said the little Jackal.

"Why, the cage he was in," said the Brahmin. "You see—"

"But I don't altogether understand," said the little Jackal. "You set him free, you say?"

"Yes, yes, yes!" said the Brahmin. "It was this way: I was walking along, and I saw the Tiger—"

"Oh, dear, dear!" interrupted the little Jackal. "I never can see through it, if you go on like that, with a long story. If you really want my opinion you must make the matter clear. What sort of cage was it?"

"Why, a big, ordinary cage, an iron cage," said the Brahmin, tugging at his beard.

"That gives me no idea at all," said the little Jackal. "See here, my friends, if we are to get on with this matter you'd best show me the spot. Then I can understand in a jiffy. Show me the cage."

So the Brahmin, the Tiger, and the little Jackal walked back together to the spot where the cage was.

"Now, let us understand the situation," said the little Jackal. "Brahmin, where were you?"

"I stood here by the roadside," said the Brahmin.

"Tiger, where were you?" asked the little Jackal.

Lesson 6: Main Character—The Protagonist

"Why, in the cage, of course," roared the Tiger.

"Oh, I beg your pardon, Father Tiger," said the little Jackal. "I really am *so* stupid; I cannot *quite* understand what happened. If you will have a little patience— *how* were you in the cage? What position were you in?"

"I stood here," said the Tiger, leaping into the cage, "with my head over my shoulder, so."

"Oh, thank you, thank you," said the little Jackal. "That makes it *much* clearer. But I still don't *quite* understand. Forgive my slow mind. Why did you not come out by yourself?"

"Can't you see that the door shut me in?" said the Tiger.

"Oh, I do beg your pardon," said the little Jackal. "I know I am very slow; I can never understand things well unless I see just how they were. If you could show me now exactly how that door works I am sure I could understand. How does it shut?"

"It shuts like this," said the Brahmin, pushing it to.

"Yes; but I don't see any lock," said the little Jackal. "Does it lock on the outside?"

"It locks like this," said the Brahmin. And he shut and bolted the door.

"Oh, does it, indeed?" said the little Jackal. "Does it, *indeed*! Well, Brother Brahmin, now that it is locked, I should advise you to let it stay locked! As for you, my friend," he said to the Tiger, "I think you will wait a good while before you'll find anyone to let you out again!"

Then he made a very low bow to the Brahmin. "Good-bye, Brother," he said. "Your way lies that way, and mine lies this. Good-bye!"

The Brahmin waved good-bye to the **wily** jackal. As his sandals clip-clopped down the dusty road, he hummed to himself and tugged at his long, white beard.

Tell It Back—Narration

1. **ORAL NARRATION**—Without looking at the text, tell the tale of *The Brahmin, the Tiger, and the Jackal* as best as you remember it using your own words. Try not to leave out any important detail.

Here is the first sentence to help you get started:

"One day in India, a Brahmin came walking down a dusty country road, his sandals clip-clopping under his feet."

2. **OUTLINE**—Create an outline for the story *The Brahmin, the Tiger, and the Jackal* using Roman numerals (*I, II, III*) for the most important events and capital letters (*A, B, C*) for less important events. Use standard numbers (*1, 2, 3*) for minor points.

I. The Brahmin releases the Tiger from his cage.
   A. The Tiger wants to eat the Brahmin.
   B. The Brahmin and the Tiger agree to ask five others if it is fair for the Tiger to eat the Brahmin.
II. They ask a Banyan Tree.
   A. The Brahmin asks the Banyan Tree for mercy.
   B. The Banyan Tree shares his complaints.
      1. Men steal my fruit.
      2. They break my twigs.
      3. They stone my branches for more fruit.
      4. They are ungrateful humans.
   C. The Tiger pounces.
      1. The Brahmin begs the Tiger to ask four others.
      2. The Tiger agrees to walk on.
III. They ask a Bullock.
   A. The Brahmin asks the Bullock for mercy.
   B. The Bullock shares his complaints.
      1. He was given no food.
      2. He was given no water.
      3. Men are thankless humans.
   C. The Tiger pounces.
      1. The Brahmin begs the Tiger to ask three others.
      2. The Tiger agrees to walk on.
IV. They ask an Eagle.
   A. The Brahmin asks the Eagle for mercy.
   B. The Eagle shares his complaints.

Lesson 6: *Main Character—The Protagonist*

1. Men stone my young.
2. They rob my eggs.
3. They shoot at me with arrows.
4. They are cruel humans.

C. The Tiger pounces.
1. The Brahmin begs the Tiger to ask two others.
2. The Tiger agrees to walk on.

V. They ask an Alligator.
A. The Brahmin asks the Alligator for mercy.
B. The Alligator shares his complaints.
1. Men hit me with stones.
2. They poke me with sharp sticks.
3. They jeer at me.
4. They are worthless humans.

C. The Tiger pounces.
1. The Brahmin begs the Tiger to ask one more.
2. The Tiger agrees to walk on.

VI. They ask a Jackal.
A. The Brahmin asks the Jackal for mercy.
B. The Jackal acts stupid and wants to see the cage.
C. The Tiger returns to the cage.
1. The Jackal asks how the cage was closed.
2. The Tiger is locked up tight.
D. The Brahmin goes on his way.

_____

_____

_____

_____

_____

_____

_____

_____

_____

Talk About It—

TE   1. Describe the character of the Brahmin. Is he someone you like or care about? Why or why not?

TE   2. Describe the character of the Tiger. Is he someone you like or care about? Why or why not?

TE   3. The characters of the Banyan Tree, Bullock, Eagle, and Alligator are all similar. How would you describe these characters?

TE   4. Describe the character of the Jackal.

TE   5. Can you name at least two of the character traits of the Brahmin? Remember that a trait is a feature of a person's character such as kindness, silliness, rudeness, sweetness, and so on. Traits also include physical features and little oddities of behavior or personality. Some people chew their fingernails as a way of showing nervousness, while others twist their hair. What traits does the Brahmin show that make him a unique character—one of a kind?

Go Deeper—

1. What kind of narrative do you think *The Brahmin, the Tiger, and the Jackal* is? (See lesson 2 to see the different categories defined again.)

   a. fable

   b. myth

   c. fairy tale

   d. history

2. Which of these proverbs would be the best moral for the tale?

   a. Too much trust makes betrayal easy.

   b. Whoever rides a tiger will find it hard to dismount.

   c. You can't chew your food with somebody else's teeth.

   d. The more danger the more honor.

3. What do you think humans can learn from the complaints of the Banyan Tree and the animals?

   Sample answer: Humans should avoid being cruel to animals and should be grateful for the help they receive.

   _____

   _____

   _____

4. <u>The moment he was out, the duplicitous Tiger sprang on the Brahmin.</u> Because the Tiger attacks the Brahmin after he says he won't, the word "duplicitous" most likely means:

   a. trustworthy

   b. ferocious

   c. untrustworthy

   d. unhelpful

5. The adjective "duplicitous" comes from the Latin word *duplus*, which means "double." The idea is that someone who is duplicitous leads a double life and can't be trusted. He appears to be a friend, but he is really an enemy. In the following list, circle some other words you could use to express this meaning.

a. double-crossing

b. honest

c. two-faced

d. treacherous

e. responsible

f. double-dealing

6. Look up the word "**gullible**" in a dictionary and write the definition.

Gullible means "easily deceived or cheated."

In a complete sentence, tell which character(s) in the story is (are) gullible and why.

Sample sentence: The Brahmin is gullible because he sets a man-eating tiger free. The Tiger is gullible because he allows the Jackal to lure him back into the cage.

Use the word "gullible" in your own complete sentence. Make sure that your sentence hints at the meaning of the word. In other words, a reader should be able to guess at what "gullible" means because of your sentence.

Sample sentence: The gullible child gave away two dimes for two nickels.

7. Look up the word "wily" in a thesaurus. Write down five synonyms here:

_ Sample synonyms: cunning, tricky, deceitful, clever, slippery _

_____

_____

In a complete sentence, tell which character in the story is wily and why.

_ Sample sentence: The Jackal is wily because he is able to trick the Tiger. _

_____

_____

Use the adjective "wily" in your own complete sentence.

_ Sample sentence: The wily girl pointed at the sky and took the little boy's lollipop.

_____

_____

Writing Time—

1. **DICTATION**—Your teacher will read a little part of *The Brahmin, the Tiger, and the Jackal* back to you. Please listen carefully! After your teacher reads once, she will read slowly again and include the punctuation marks. Your task will be to write down the sentences as your teacher reads them one by one.

_ Modify according to student level. Note that dictations are not spelling tests. Difficult words can be spelled on the board prior to dictation.

The Eagle soared slowly overhead a moment, then he came lower and spoke in a thin, clear voice.

"Tiger, where were you?" asked the little Jackal.

_____

_____

_____

Lesson 6: *Main Character—The Protagonist*

2. **SENTENCE PLAY**—A comparison using the words "like" or "as" is called a **simile** (sim-eh-lee). "My love is like a red, red rose" is a simile because it compares love with a red rose and uses the word "like." "The girl was as brown as chocolate ice cream" is a simile because it compares a girl's skin color to chocolate ice cream and it uses the word "as."

A. The Alligator in the story says, "I lie here in the mud all day as harmless as a pigeon." What might the Alligator have said if he were to brag about being dangerous? Think of two comparisons.

"I lie here in the mud all day as dangerous as a _____

_ Sample sentence: I lie here in the mud all day as dangerous as a rattlesnake. _____."

"I lie here in the mud all day as dangerous as a _____

_ Sample sentence: I lie here in the mud all day as dangerous as a scorpion. _____."

B. Following the same pattern, what might a parrot say about herself? Parrots don't lie in mud all day, so you'll need to come up with something different.

I ____ Sample sentence: I perch here in the _____ here in the
trees all day as pretty as a flower.

_____ all day as

_____ as a

_____ .

C. Following the same pattern, create your own new sentence comparing an animal to something else.

___ Sample sentence for a snake: I slither in the grass all day as quiet as a breeze. _____

_____

_____

_____

3. **COPIOUSNESS**—Here is the famous sentence used by Erasmus in his book of rhetoric, *De Duplici Copia Verborum ac Rerum*, which means "On the Twofold Abundance of Expressions and Ideas": "Your letter pleased me greatly."

A. Circle the following sentences that have roughly the same meaning as Erasmus's sentence. The words "missive" and "epistle" are synonyms for the word "letter."

1. Your note delighted me very much.
2. Receiving your letter made me very happy.
3. As a result of your letter, I was filled with gladness.
4. Your epistle gave me sweet feelings.
5. Your letter brought a frown to my face.
6. The arrival of your letter gave me a thrill of joy.
7. Because of your letter, I found myself rejoicing.
8. The missive you sent flooded my heart with happiness.
9. Because of your letter, I felt gloomy for days.
10. What wonders of delight did your epistle give me!
11. Your letter affected me with transports of joy.
12. I rejoiced greatly when your letter arrived.
13. Your missive gave me such rapture and joy.
14. Never have I felt so terrible as when your letter arrived.

B. Now write two new variations of the sentence, "Your letter pleased me greatly."

1. _____ Sample variations:
Your letter brought me tremendous gladness.
_____ Such delight did I feel when I received your note. _____

2. _____

_____

C. Mark the nouns (there are three), adjectives (there are four), and verbs (there are two) in the following sentence. Place an *N* over the nouns, *ADJ* over the adjectives, and *V* over the verbs.

- Remember that a noun is a person, place, thing, or idea. Examples: police officer, park, slide, fun
- An adjective describes a noun. Examples: purple, nasty, sweet, tiny, round
- A verb is often the action word of the sentence. Examples: run, slide, kick, dance, fly, fall, bump, laugh, cry

N		V			ADJ	ADJ	N	V		ADJ	ADJ	N

A Brahmin came walking down a dusty country road, tugging at his long, white beard.

As you change the sentence as directed in the following exercise, try to come up with six variations, all keeping nearly the same meaning as the original sentence.

D. Replace the nouns and verbs with synonyms. You don't need to change the noun "Brahmin," but you can call him "a Hindu priest" if you wish.

> Sample sentence: A Hindu priest came strolling down a dusty, country lane pulling at his long, white chin hair.

_____

_____

_____

E. Replace only the four adjectives. They do not have to be synonyms.

> Sample sentence: A Brahmin came walking down a dirty, empty road, tugging at his wild, gray beard.

_____

_____

_____

Lesson 6: *Main Character—The Protagonist*

F. Change the end of the sentence using the suggestions given. Your new sentence should still make sense.

   i. Walking down a dusty country road, _____

   > Sample sentence: Walking down a dusty country road, a Brahmin came tugging at his long, white beard.

   _____.

   ii. Tugging at his long, white beard, _____

   > Sample sentence: Tugging at his long, white beard, a Brahmin came down a dusty country road.

   _____

4. **CHANGE THE DIALOGUE**—*The Brahmin, the Tiger, and the Jackal* contains a good deal of dialogue. Remember that dialogue is a conversation between two or more people and it makes a story more interesting. Dialogue can also make the protagonist more attractive to your readers, as well as more quirky or unique.

From the following sentence you can tell that the Brahmin is a humble and peaceful man, and also a bit gullible: <u>"But, Brother Tiger," said the Brahmin as his bony knees knocked together, "you promised you would not. It is not fair or just that you should eat me, when I set you free."</u>

A. Rewrite the dialogue as if there is a new protagonist who is a super-strong superhero with bulging muscles. The Tiger has just sprung from the cage and wants to devour the superhero. What would the superhero tell the Tiger?

   > Sample dialogue: "Listen, Tiger," said the superhero, "if you try to bite me, I'm going to feed you all of your teeth."

   _____

   _____

   _____

   _____

B. Rewrite the dialogue as if the protagonist were a fearless and scolding old lady. What would she tell a roaring Tiger?

> Sample dialogue: "You'd better get away from me, Sonny," scolded the old lady, "or I'm going to whack you with my umbrella."

_____

_____

_____

_____

5. **CHANGE THE POINT OF VIEW**—The story about the Brahmin is told in the third-person point of view, using the pronouns "he," "she," "it," and "they." Tell the beginning of the story in the first-person point of view (using "I" and "we"), as if you, the storyteller, are the Brahmin. Feel free to add your thoughts and feelings. How does the change in voice affect the story? **TE**

One day in India, a Brahmin came walking down a dusty country road, his sandals clip-clopping under his feet. As he walked along, he hummed to himself and tugged thoughtfully at his long, white beard.

Presently, the Brahmin came upon a Tiger shut up in a strong iron cage. The villagers had caught him and shut him up there for his wickedness.

"Oh, good Brahmin, kind Brahmin," said the Tiger, "please let me out to get a little drink! I am so thirsty, and there is no water here."

"But Brother Tiger," said the Brahmin, tugging at his beard, "you know if I should let you out, you would spring on me and eat me up."

"Never, dear Brahmin!" said the Tiger. "Never in the world would I do such an ungrateful thing! Never would I dream of double-crossing you! Just let me out a little minute, to get a little, little drink of water, sweet Brahmin!"

Now the Brahmin was a kind-hearted man and believed that the animals were his brothers. So he unlocked the door and let the Tiger out. The moment he was out, the duplicitous Tiger sprang on the Brahmin and was about to eat him up.

Lesson 6: *Main Character—The Protagonist*

"But, Brother Tiger," said the Brahmin as his bony knees knocked together, "you promised you would not. It is not fair or just that you should eat me, when I set you free."

"It is perfectly right and just," said the Tiger, "and I shall eat you up."

Sample rewrite:

One day in India, I came walking down a dusty country road, my sandals clip-clopping under my feet. As I walked along, I hummed to myself and tugged thoughtfully at my long, white beard.

Presently, I came upon a Tiger shut up in a strong iron cage. The villagers had caught him and shut him up there for his wickedness.

"Oh, good Brahmin, kind Brahmin," said the Tiger to me, "please let me out to get a little drink! I am so thirsty, and there is no water here."

"But Brother Tiger," said I, tugging at my beard, "you know if I should let you out you would spring on me and eat me up." And so on.

6. **CHANGE THE PROTAGONIST**—What if the Brahmin were not a Brahmin but an entirely different character? How would the story change, for instance, if the protagonist were a salesman, a teacher, or a lazy person? When creating a new character, it is often helpful to make a list of traits to help guide his or her development. In the following spaces, brainstorm a list of traits for a new character.

My New Character

Full name:

_____

Male or female:

_____

Race or ethnicity:

_____

Age in years:

_____

Age description (circle): baby, toddler, kid, tween, teenager, young adult, adult, senior, elder

Height and weight in numbers:

_____

Height and weight description (circle): short, squat, small, puny, tiny, delicate, tall, hulking, lanky, lean, skinny, wiry, angular, slender, medium, trim, brawny, beefy, burly, sturdy, slim, spare, stout, stocky, big, portly, chubby, fat, pudgy

Hair and eye color:

_____

Hair description (circle): straight, curly, wavy, kinked, spiky, soft, velvety, springy, thick, frizzy, short, long, ropy, shaved, bald

Lesson 6: Main Character—The Protagonist

Eye description (circle): round, narrow, almond, puffy, droopy, bleary, red, tired, heavy, deep, dancing, flashing, glinting, sparkling, twinkling, stony

Distinct physical traits, such as voice, health, size of nose, missing limbs or eyes, glasses, moles, warts, or wrinkles

_____

Character Quirks (oddities of behavior)

Odd tastes in clothing:

_____

Style of walking or talking:

_____

Eating habits or tastes:

_____

Good habits:

_____

Bad habits:

_____

Character Occupation

What does your character do for a living? Some possibilities include: mother, father, grocer, butcher, baker, blacksmith, hunter, fisherman, farmer, wood cutter, policeman, fireman, soldier, sailor, waiter, waitress, doctor, lawyer, banker, merchant, errand boy, errand girl, messenger, fish seller, fruit seller, cobbler (shoe maker), tailor (clothes maker), shepherd, drover (livestock mover), cowboy, cowgirl, druggist (pharmacist), robber, thief, student, musician, juggler, mason (stonecutter), preacher, rabbi, priest, miller, mudlark (sewer cleaner), chimney sweep

_____

Character Adjectives

Use adjectives to describe your character. Remember that a protagonist should have some likeable qualities. Here are a few to consider: cheerful, lazy, shy, proud, polite, lonely, friendly, silly, bossy, grumpy, gentle, loving, messy, stupid, brave, clumsy, sneaky, saintly, innocent, sweet.

_____

Now that you have filled in your survey of character traits and quirks, you are ready to rewrite the beginning of *The Brahmin, the Tiger, and the Jackal* with a new character. Be sure to give your character a new name, occupation, and manner of talking and walking.

One day in India, a Brahmin came walking down a dusty country road, his sandals clip-clopping under his feet. As he walked along, he hummed to himself and tugged thoughtfully at his long, white beard.

Presently, the Brahmin came upon a Tiger shut up in a strong iron cage. The villagers had caught him and shut him up there for his wickedness.

"Oh, good Brahmin, kind Brahmin," said the Tiger, "please let me out to get a little drink! I am so thirsty, and there is no water here."

"But Brother Tiger," said the Brahmin, tugging at his beard, "you know if I should let you out, you would spring on me and eat me up."

"Never, dear Brahmin!" said the Tiger. "Never in the world would I do such an ungrateful thing! Never would I dream of double-crossing you! Just let me out a little minute, to get a little, little drink of water, sweet Brahmin!"

Now the Brahmin was a kind-hearted man and believed that the animals were his brothers. So he unlocked the door and let the Tiger out. The moment he was out, the duplicitous Tiger sprang on the Brahmin and was about to eat him up.

"But, Brother Tiger," said the Brahmin as his bony knees knocked together, "you promised you would not. It is not fair or just that you should eat me, when I set you free."

"It is perfectly right and just," said the Tiger, "and I shall eat you up."

Lesson 6: *Main Character—The Protagonist*

Sample rewrite:

One day in America, a salesman came strutting down a smooth city road, his shiny leather shoes squeaking under his feet. As he walked along, he talked to himself about winning the salesman of the year award and brushed back his black hair with his hand.

Presently, the salesman came upon a Tiger shut up in a strong circus cage. The circus performers had shut him up there because he ate the animal trainer.

"Oh, good salesman, kind salesman," said the Tiger, "please let me out to get a little drink! I am so thirsty, and there is no water here."

"Well, hello there Tiger," said the salesman, combing his fingers through his hair, "I'll let you out of there, buddy, ol' pal o' mine, if I can sell you a new suit. That stripy thing you're wearing is totally out of style. But, hey now, you're not thinking of eating me, are you?"

"Never, dear salesman!" said the Tiger. "Never in the world would I do such an ungrateful thing! Never would I dream of double crossing you! Just let me out a little minute, to get a little, little drink of water, sweet salesman!"

Now the salesman was certainly hoping to sell the Tiger a new suit, and maybe a fingernail file for his claws. So he unlocked the door and let the Tiger out. The moment he was out, the duplicitous Tiger sprang on the salesman and was about to eat him up.

"Wow, Tiger," said the salesman and he cleared his throat impressively, "if you eat me, my friend, you won't get the latest and greatest outfits for big cats like you. You don't want to be seen as a schlub by the lady Tigers do you? Why, they wouldn't even give you a second glance in that orange-and-black number you're wearing."

Speak It— 🎙

Both of these exercises provide valuable additional practice with dialogue. The process of copying down actual interactions will show students that real conversation does not necessarily translate to interesting literary dialogue. On the other hand, changing the protagonist in the sample story will significantly impact the texture of that character's speech.

1. Listen carefully to a conversation in your home or school and write it down as the people are speaking. Expand or amplify the dialogue and read it aloud in class as a conversation with a fellow student. Before you act out any conversation, however, make sure that you have the speakers' permission to share the conversation. You don't want to embarrass anyone!

2. To a classmate, read your changes to the protagonist in *The Brahmin, the Tiger, and the Jackal.* Have you improved the story in any way? If you're a solo student, use a recording device to record yourself and play it back.

Lesson 6: Main Character—The Protagonist

Talk About It—

1. The Brahmin seems to be a kind and gentle man because he sets the fierce Tiger free. He is also a bit naïve, which means that he lacks experience with the world. No experienced person would set a man-eating Tiger free. Most people would say that they like kind people because kind people treat others well.

2. The Tiger is not only fierce, but he is a traitor as well. It shows bad character that the Tiger would kill the one man who set him free from his cage. Most people would say that the Tiger is not someone they like or care about. He would be a dangerous friend.

3. All of these creatures have bitter feelings toward human beings. They have no pity for the Brahmin even though he is not the kind of person who would hurt them.

4. The Jackal is a wily, clever character. He acts foolish, but his goal is to trick the Tiger and get him back in its cage.

5. The Brahmin tugs at his beard, wears clip-clopping sandals, and has bony knees that knock, and he calls animals "Brother."

Writing Time—

5. First person narration often helps us to be more sympathetic with the narrator. We see the narrator much more "up close and personal," and we tend to relate better to his or her problems.

Notes

The purpose of this lesson is to introduce the idea of an opposing character (antagonist) as well as to remind students of the importance of conflict to a story.

In this lesson, your students will practice:
- written narration
- outlining
- critical thinking
- writing with strings of adjectives
- replacing lackluster adjectives with specific adjectives
- amplification
- dialogue and monologue

Lesson 7

Opposing Character— The Antagonist

In the last lesson I mentioned that you can hold your reader's attention in the middle of the story if you have interesting characters and conflict. The word "conflict" comes from the very useful Latin verb *confligere*, which means "to strike together." So conflict can be any sort of striking together or clash, whether it's a quarrel or a duel or a full-blown war. I don't know what it is about human nature, but people find conflict enjoyable—as long as they're at a safe distance from it.

Look at the stories you've read so far in this book. They all have conflict in the middle.

▶ What is the conflict in *The Fifth Labor of Hercules*? **TE**

▶ What is the conflict in *The Brahmin, the Tiger, and the Jackal*? **TE**

In both stories there is a person or animal that causes conflict for the main character. This conflict-causing person is known as the **antagonist**. The antagonist goes against the protagonist. Think of the antagonist as the anti-protagonist.

Protagonist=the main character

Antagonist=the anti-protagonist, the opposing character

What is the result when a protagonist and an antagonist strike against each other? Conflict, of course! Like steel striking flint, the protagonist and the antagonist together cause sparks to fly.

In addition to conflict, your main character needs a goal to be interesting. In other words, he must want to reach a certain end. All main characters, that is all protagonists, must have a goal in mind. A protagonist might want to reach the top of a mountain or survive a terrible blizzard. He might want to learn to fly a kite or play the piano. He might want to slay a dragon, win the love of a girl, or win a race around the world. What does the character want to achieve? Whatever it is, that is his goal.

Ah, but reaching the goal can't be too easy! Your story will be most interesting if the protagonist's goal is just out of reach. Just as it looks like the protagonist might get what he most desires, his goal is snatched away from him. When a story character wants something, the antagonist gets in the way and the conflict begins.

Do you know the story of *The Wonderful Wizard of Oz*? Dorothy, a girl from Kansas, gets carried off by a cyclone and deposited in the magical land of Oz. All she wants to do is return to her Aunt Em and Uncle Henry at their farm in Kansas. Unfortunately, a fearsome antagonist stands in the way of this goal: the Wicked Witch of the West. The Wicked Witch does everything in her power to capture Dorothy and steal her silver slippers. She sends wolves, crows, bees, and Winkie soldiers to attack her. At last, she summons flying monkeys, and these brutes grab the poor girl and carry her to the witch's castle. Dorothy escapes by sheer accident: She throws a bucket of water at her antagonist, and the witch and all of her "beautiful wickedness" melts away. *The Wonderful Wizard of Oz* contains the perfect example of a protagonist who is frustrated by an antagonist as she pursues her goal.

Strange as it may seem, an antagonist does not always have to be a human being. Sometimes it can be a wild animal or nature itself. Pretend your protagonist is a mountain climber, trying to reach the top of one of the great Himalayan Mountains. Along the way, she could get buried in an avalanche or fall down a deep crack in a glacier (called a crevasse). She could get attacked by a mountain goat or an eagle. The weather might change and a storm might strike just as she reaches the peak. Nature can be a fierce antagonist. Even though nature is not a human being with an active hatred of people, sometimes it can seem to act with human cruelty. Any natural disaster like a blizzard, a tornado, or a tsunami seems almost to be alive and hateful.

Sometimes the antagonist is not just one person but many people. The story you are about to read describes a famous incident in the life of Julius Caesar. As you read, try to guess who the antagonists are. What is Caesar's goal, and how do the antagonists get in his way?

A narrative based on fact is called **nonfiction**, whereas **fiction** is the name for any imaginary story. After reading the story through once or twice, use a highlighter to mark parts of the story that seem like *nonfiction* (fact). Use a different color highlighter to mark the parts of the story that seem like *fiction* (make-believe). You might notice that the parts where Julius Caesar acts in a foolhardy manner seem imaginary, as if the author is trying too hard to prove his courage. **A**

> **A**Remind students that history is a form of narrative. It contains a plot line (beginning, middle, and end) as well as characters drawn from real life.

nonfictional/factual

fictional/imaginary **B**

B The skill of discerning between fiction and nonfiction has some subjective elements, so student answers may vary.

Julius Caesar and the Pirates

—adapted from *Old World Hero Stories* by Eva March Tappan, *The Story of Rome* by Mary Macgregor, and *The Children's Plutarch: Tales of the Romans* by F.J. Gould

"I am a Roman!"

"A Roman, sir? We beg your pardon, sir. O, kind Roman, forgive us for making you walk the plank!"

With this mockery, the pirates pushed the poor sailor into the sea and he was promptly drowned.

Julius Caesar watched it happen, but he was by nature as fierce as the pirates who had taken his ship. He showed no fear as they approached him.

"How much money can we get for this wealthy **patrician**?" the pirates asked each other, brandishing their knives. "He might be worth maybe twenty talents."

"Twenty talents," Caesar scoffed. "You should ask at least fifty."

Fifty talents! That was a king's ransom!

"Very well," the pirates said. "We'll ask for fifty. But if we don't get that much, your life won't be worth a spit in the sea."

Lesson 7: *Opposing Character—The Antagonist*

And so young Julius Caesar, at the age of twenty-three, was taken captive by pirates.

These sea-robbers came from Cilicia, a province of Asia Minor, where they had whole villages and towns in their possession, as well as castles on the hilltops. Large numbers of persons who were discontented with Roman rule joined the roving warriors of the sea, and their galleys swarmed all over the Mediterranean. They made sudden attacks on cities on the coast and at one place seized and carried off two officers (**prætors**) and their servants. They plundered the holy temples of Apollo and other gods. Purple awnings shaded their ships. The back parts were gilded with gold, the oars were plated with silver, and bands of musicians played while the pirates drank and danced.

When Julius Caesar was taken by Cilician pirates, he was on his way to the island of Rhodes to study rhetoric. Someday he hoped to become a great speaker, a man who could sway crowds of people. He had dreams of being elected consul, the highest public office in the Roman Republic, which is something like the presidency of the United States.

It was near the Greek island of Pharmakonisi that the sea robbers seized his ship and drowned some of the crew. Caesar was forced to send his followers away to raise the ransom money.

Caesar knew that the pirates often put their prisoners to death. Now alone with them, he decided that they would treat him better if he never winced at their knives, never blinked at their mockery. For thirty-eight days he lived with them, sometimes amusing himself by joining in their sports, sometimes reading to them poems he had written or rehearsing speeches he had prepared.

To these speeches they would listen, but without giving any applause. Then Caesar would grow angry with them, calling them names and berating them for their stupidity. "You don't know poetry when you hear it," he said. "You think you can scoff at my verses and orations because I am your prisoner. I'll take you prisoners some day, and then you shall have your pay."

"What will it be?" they demanded with shouts of laughter.

"I'll crucify every one of you," he replied quietly, but they only laughed all the more.

At other times, if Caesar wished to sleep and the pirates were carousing late in the night, drinking and singing, he would tell them to be quiet.

The pirates mocked the strange ways and words of their captive and paid no heed to his threats. Sometimes they would tell him to hold his tongue or they would kill him.

But Caesar was earnest when angry. No sooner was his ransom paid and he set free than the first thing he did was to hire ships to go in search of these very same pirates. He soon found and captured them, and in the end he crucified them, as he had threatened to do.

Caesar then journeyed to Rhodes to study rhetoric. He certainly profited by his studies, for on his return to Rome his **eloquence** won him fame.

Talk About It—

TE 1. Who is the protagonist (the main character) in this story and what is his goal? Who are the antagonists and how do they interrupt the protagonist from reaching his goals?

TE 2. What are some things that the pirates could have done to make it harder, but not impossible, for Julius Caesar to reach his goal?

TE 3. What does the author do to make the beginning of the story interesting?

TE 4. Piracy is still a problem in the world today. Why do you think some people become pirates?

Tell It Back—Narration

1. Written narration:

   A. Write your own sentence to tell what happens at the beginning of the story.

   Sample sentence: The pirates capture a ship carrying Julius Caesar and drown some sailors.

   _____

   _____

   _____

Lesson 7: Opposing Character—The Antagonist

B. Write your own sentence to tell what happens in the middle of the story.

Sample sentence: Caesar treats the pirates just as fiercely as they treat him, and he forces them to hear his speeches.

_____

_____

_____

C. Write a sentence to tell what happens at the end of the story.

Sample sentence: Once Caesar's ransom is paid, he hunts down the pirates and crucifies them.

_____

_____

_____

2. Outline: Create an outline for *Julius Caesar and the Pirates* using Roman numerals (*I, II, III*) for the most important events and capital letters (*A, B, C*) for less important events. Use standard numbers (*1, 2, 3*) for minor points.

> I. Julius Caesar is captured by Cilician pirates.
>   A. Sailors are drowned.
>   B. Out of pride, Caesar demands the pirates request a higher ransom.
> II. Caesar lives with the pirates.
>   A. He plays in their games.
>   B. He gives them speeches.
>   C. He mocks them for their stupidity.
>   D. He threatens to crucify them.
> III. Caesar is ransomed and returns to Cilicia.
>   A. He captures the pirates.
>   B. He crucifies them as promised.

_____

_____

_____

_____

_____

_____

_____

_____

_____

_____

_____

_____

_____

_____

Go Deeper—

1. What kind of narrative do you think *Julius Caesar and the Pirates* mostly is?

    (See lesson 2 to see the different categories defined again.)

    a. fable

    b. myth

    c. fairy tale

    d. history

2. Use the context of the sentence to guess the meaning of the word **patrician**:

    "How much money can we get for this wealthy patrician?" "Patrician"

    probably means:

    a. a Roman farmer

    b. a Roman student

    c. a Roman noble

    d. a Roman athlete

Lesson 7: Opposing Character—The Antagonist

3. The word "eloquence" derives from the Latin prefix *ex-*, which means "out," and the verb *loqui*, which means "to speak." In other words: "to speak out." But "eloquence" is a noun, not a verb. If Caesar won fame for his eloquence, what do you think is the best meaning of "eloquence"?

   a. skillful and persuasive speech

   b. silly and foolish speech

   c. weak and useless speech

   d. patriotic speech

4. The character of Julius Caesar in this story seems mixed, both admirable and unworthy. What is something Caesar does that is admirable? What is something Caesar does that seems unworthy?

   Caesar's courage in the face of danger is admirable. The way he treats the pirates so rudely shows that he can be selfish himself, which is unworthy. And did the pirates deserve to be killed by crucifixion for not enjoying his poems? Certainly not; crucifixion is a very cruel form of execution whereby the criminal is nailed with spikes to a cross of wood. However, it would not be an unusual punishment in that time given their criminal activity (piracy) and the fact that they had crossed Caesar, a powerful man.

Writing Time— ⏱

1. **DICTATION**—Your teacher will read a little part of *Julius Caesar and the Pirates* back to you. Please listen carefully! After your teacher reads once, she will read slowly again and include the punctuation marks. Your task will be to write down the sentences as your teacher reads them one by one.

> Modify according to student level. Note that dictations are not spelling tests. Difficult words can be spelled on the board prior to dictation.
>
> 💬 "Twenty talents," Caesar scoffed. "You should ask at least fifty."
>
> 💬 When Julius Caesar was taken by Cilician pirates, he was on his way to the island of Rhodes to study rhetoric.

2. **SENTENCE PLAY**—You already know that adjectives describe nouns in a sentence. Sometimes a noun needs to be explained by another noun or a whole noun phrase. Here are two examples from the story about Julius Caesar:

- <u>These sea-robbers came from Cilicia [noun], a province of Asia Minor [noun phrase].</u> The phrase "a province of Asia Minor" explains what Cilicia is.
- <u>Someday he hoped to become a great speaker [noun], a man who could sway crowds of people [noun phrase].</u> The phrase "a man who could sway crowds of people" explains what a great speaker is.

Now it's your turn. Fill in the blank after the nouns in the following exercises by providing another noun or a noun phrase to explain it. Use a comma to separate the noun and the noun phrase. For example:

I was chased down the street by Fang.

I was chased down the street by Fang, my pet rattlesnake.

A. It was a happy book, a book about _____

> Sample sentence: It was a happy book, a book about finding treasure at the bottom of the sea.

Lesson 7: *Opposing Character—The Antagonist*

B. Everyone should visit _____, a place famous

for __ Sample sentence: Everyone should visit Los Angeles, a place famous for Mexican __.
cantinas and beautiful beaches.

C. Our house was hit by a tornado, _____

__ Sample sentence: Our house was hit by a tornado, a swirling cloud of powerful winds. __.

D. You should meet our neighbor Gertrude, _____

__ Sample sentence: You should meet our neighbor Gertrude, an old lady who drives a red Ferrari. __.

E. She was stung by an insect, _____

__ Sample sentence: She was stung by an insect, an orange-colored fire ant. __.

3. **COPIOUSNESS—**

A. Study the photo of the bust of Julius
Caesar for a moment. Write down at
least six adjectives to describe this bust
and the expression on Caesar's face.

__ Sample answers: thoughtful, serious, stern, __
proud, fierce, angry, mean, ruthless, relent-
less, determined, arrogant, intense

_____

_____

_____

_____

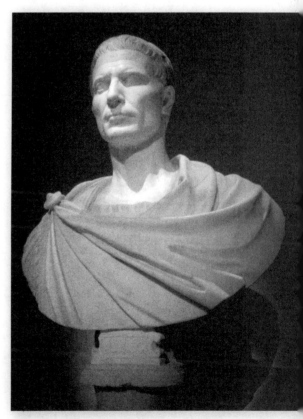

▲ Bust of Julius Caesar

B. Adjectives can often be strung together, separated by commas. For example: "The muddy, old, green river gurgled through the canyon." String together three of your adjectives from the last exercise to describe the look upon Julius Caesar's face and rewrite the following complete sentence. Keep in mind that the noun you are describing is "look."

Caesar wore a look upon his face.

_____ Sample sentence: Caesar wore a serious, intense, proud look upon his face. _____

_____

C. The following sentences refer to the Roman historian Suetonius and to his description of various Roman emperors. Create a string of three adjectives to describe the underlined noun in each sentence and rewrite the sentence.

   i. Suetonius portrays Augustus as a handsome <u>man</u>.

   _____ Sample sentence: Suetonius portrays Augustus as a handsome, strong, muscular, _____
   nearsighted man.
   _____

   ii. Suetonius tells us that Caligula smelled like a <u>goat</u>.

   _____ Sample sentence: Suetonius tells us that Caligula smelled like a filthy, hairy, nasty goat. _____

   _____

   iii. Suetonius describes Nero as having a big <u>belly</u> and skinny <u>legs</u>.

   _____ Sample sentence: Suetonius describes Nero as having a big, monstrous, bulbous, _____
   pink belly and skinny, scrawny, hairy, dirty legs.
   _____

D. An adjective such as "good" is often weak because it is not very descriptive. For example:
   "I had a good day."
   "Really? Why was it good?"
   "I ate apple pie today."
   "Oh! So you had a delicious day!"

Lesson 7: Opposing Character—The Antagonist

The underlined adjectives in the following sentences are all weak. They are not specific or descriptive. Your job is to intensify the underlined adjectives. This means that you should choose an adjective that is similar, but more descriptive and strong, than the adjective provided. Use a thesaurus only if you get stuck.

Example: Julius Caesar rode a <u>good</u> horse.

Julius Caesar rode a swift horse.

Notice, in this example, that "swift" is a much more specific word than "good." "Good" could refer to almost anything. The horse could be good because it obeyed or because it had good breeding. The word "swift" tells us that the horse is good because it could run fast.

As you intensify the following sentences, remember to rewrite them as complete sentences.

i. The Romans kept <u>big</u> dogs known as Molossus dogs.

   Sample sentence: The Romans kept heavy dogs known as Molossus dogs.

_____

ii. Queen Zenobia of Palmyra was a <u>good</u> warrior.

   Sample sentence: Queen Zenobia of Palmyra was a clever warrior.

_____

iii. No dessert in ancient Rome was as <u>nice</u> as a pastry called *spira*.

   Sample sentence: No dessert in ancient Rome was as sweet as a pastry called *spira*.

_____

iv. Rome is a beautiful city because of its <u>pretty</u> marble.

   Sample sentence: Rome is a beautiful city because of its white marble.

_____

v. The eruption of Mount Vesuvius, a volcano in Italy, caused a <u>bad</u> disaster in AD 79.

> Sample sentence: The eruption of Mount Vesuvius, a volcano in Italy, caused a massive disaster in AD 79.

4. **AMPLIFICATION—**

A. Add dialogue and description to the following story fragments to show how ruthless and fierce the pirates are. When adding dialogue, be clear about who is speaking. Also, add a description of the pirates.

"I am a Roman!"

"A Roman, sir? We beg your pardon, sir. O, kind Roman, forgive us for making you walk the plank!"

With this mockery, the pirates pushed the poor sailor into the sea and he was promptly drowned.

> Sample amplification:
>
> The pirates who surrounded the sailor were a ragged, nasty bunch. Many of them had wicked scars from knife fights and bloodshot eyes, spiky beards, and yellow teeth. They smelled of garlic and twenty-year-old cheese. "Walk the plank!" they shouted.
>
> The sailor, an officer of the ship, tried to impress the pirates. "I am a Roman."
>
> "A Roman, sir?" the pirates said with a bow. "O, pardon us. A thousand pardons. We won't make you walk the plank after all."
>
> True to their word, the pirates grabbed the poor sailor and threw him bodily into the dark blue sea.

[Julius Caesar] was by nature as fierce as the pirates who had taken his ship. He showed no fear as they approached him.

> Sample amplification:
>
> One pirate with a peg leg approached Julius Caesar with a long, blood-stained sword in his hand. He wore a cruel, gap-toothed grin on his face. "Now for you, patrician. What if I skin you alive?"
>
> "Oh, fine," Caesar said carelessly. He looked at the man as if he were looking at a bug that needed to be squashed. "Skin me if you must. You must not care about becoming rich, for you would become very rich if you demanded a ransom for me."

B. Add dialogue to the following sentence to show what might have been said between Caesar and the pirates. <u>At other times, if Caesar wished to sleep and the pirates were carousing late in the night, drinking and singing, he would tell them to be quiet.</u>

> Sample amplification:
>
> "Did you just tell us to be quiet?" the pirates demanded.
>
> "I did," Caesar replied, "and if I have to hear any more of your stupid songs, I'm going to throw a rock at you."
>
> The pirates thought that this was all very amusing. "It's a pity we didn't drown you!" they shouted playfully.
>
> "I agree," Caesar shouted back. "Then my ears would be stuffed with water, and I wouldn't have to listen to your horrible singing. You sound like a bunch of plucked parrots."
>
> At this, the pirates laughed and jeered and then kept on singing. But Caesar was not smiling, and he vowed to himself to get revenge.

C. Instead of writing a dialogue this time, write a monologue, as if Julius Caesar is only muttering to himself or whispering fiercely to himself about the pirates' behavior. Use the following sentence to set your scene: <u>At other times, if Caesar wished to sleep and the pirates were carousing late in the night, drinking and singing, he would tell them to be quiet.</u>

> Sample amplification:
>
> "Ugh! I can't take this rotten singing and drinking any more. The more they drink, the worse they sing. If only I had a cohort of Roman soldiers, I would clean this town out and not one of these knuckleheads would be left to stink up the air. No! Don't sing '100 Bottles of Beer on the Wall'! Not again! Argh! When my ransom is paid, I will come back here! As sure as my name is Julius Caesar, I'll come back here and clap every one of these idiots in irons!"

_____

_____

_____

_____

_____

D. After he crucifies the pirates, Julius Caesar again sets sail to study rhetoric on the island of Rhodes. Think of at least five other antagonists that could stand in the way of Julius Caesar's arrival on the island and write them as a list. Remember that an antagonist does not have to be a human being.

> Sample answers:
>
> a storm
> a sea monster
> a war
> a traitor on board the ship
> sickness
> a volcano
> a tidal wave

Speak It— 🎙️

Rhetoric has the power to change people's minds. Perhaps Julius Caesar was able to persuade the pirates to spare his life through his use of rhetoric. Sadly, we have no record of his speeches to them.

You are about to read a magnificent speech by William Shakespeare, a speech that is famous for its rhetoric. In this scene, Julius Caesar has just been murdered by senators who were afraid that he was seeking to be the one and only ruler of the Roman Republic. Mark Antony, friend of Julius Caesar, is able to persuade Roman crowds to turn against the senators who murdered him.

Team up in groups of three. One student will introduce the speech, and the other two will deliver it by reading at the podium.

Remember elocution! In a dramatic reading, it is vital that you speak

- with volume. Everyone in the room should be able to hear you.
- with drama. You should sound sad when the words call for sorrow, angry when the words call for anger. Any emotion in the text should find its way into your voice.
- with gestures. Gestures accentuate the emotions in your voice and make the reading even more dramatic.
- with pauses. Never read quickly without taking a breath. Pauses help to accent your emotions like gestures.

Introduction—Each student should write an introductory paragraph that includes the following facts:

- *The Tragedy of Julius Caesar* is a play written by William Shakespeare.
- It was probably first performed in 1599.
- Julius Caesar seized control of the Roman government and became "dictator for life." A dictator is a ruler who holds all the power in a government.
- Mark Antony, Caesar's loyal friend and cousin, delivers this speech after Caesar is stabbed to death in the Roman Senate. The senators feared that Caesar would destroy the Roman Republic and make it his own kingdom. The leader of the assassins was a senator named Brutus.

Lesson 7: Opposing Character—The Antagonist   111

- Antony is trying to persuade Roman citizens that Caesar was an innocent victim of Brutus. By repeating, "Brutus is an honorable man," Antony is being sarcastic. He is really saying the opposite, that Brutus is a dishonorable man.

Antony—Reader One

Friends, Romans, countrymen, lend me your ears.
I come to bury Caesar, not to praise him.
The evil that men do lives after them;
The good is oft **interred** with their bones.
So let it be with Caesar. The noble Brutus
Hath told you Caesar was ambitious.
If it were so, it was a grievous fault,
And grievously hath Caesar answered it.
Here, under leave of Brutus and the rest—
For Brutus is an honorable man;
So are they all, all honorable men—
Come I to speak in Caesar's funeral.
He was my friend, faithful and just to me.
But Brutus says he was ambitious,
And Brutus is an honorable man.

Antony—Reader Two

He hath brought many captives home to Rome
Whose ransoms did the general **coffers** fill.
Did this in Caesar seem ambitious?
When that the poor have cried, Caesar hath wept.
Ambition should be made of sterner stuff.
Yet Brutus says he was ambitious,
And Brutus is an honorable man.
You all did see that on the **Lupercal**

Lesson 7: Opposing Character—The Antagonist

Lesson 7: Opposing Character—The Antagonist

▶ What is the conflict in *The Fifth Labor of Hercules*?
Though the stable is not a person, Hercules first has a conflict with it. He must "fight" with the stable in order to overcome its filth. Next he has conflict with King Augeas because the king refuses to honor his promise.

▶ What is the conflict in *The Brahmin, the Tiger, and the Jackal*?
The Tiger betrays the Brahmin's trust and wants to eat him.

Talk About It—

1. Julius Caesar is the protagonist, and his goal is to reach the island of Rhodes to study rhetoric. The antagonists are the pirates who take him captive, thus preventing him from making it to Rhodes.

2. They could have forced Caesar to become a slave or a pirate. They could have raised the price of his ransom.

3. The author starts with dialogue right in the middle of the action. A Roman sailor is about to walk the plank.

4. Some people are forced to become pirates by other pirates. Some people have trouble making a living and become pirates to make their fortunes. Other people are greedy and enjoy the life of stealing from the weak. The author of this story tells us that some people became pirates because they were discontented with Roman rule.

Notes

_____

_____

_____

_____

_____

_____

_____

_____

_____

_____

_____

_____

_____

_____

_____

_____

The purpose of this lesson is to introduce history as a form of narrative and for students to begin to distinguish between fact and opinion.

In this lesson, your students will practice:

- written narration
- critical thinking
- replacing lackluster nouns with specific nouns
- summarizing a historical narrative
- amplifying a historical narrative
- distinguishing fact from fiction

Lesson 8 ·

Historical Narrative

You know already that history is a type of narrative. It contains both a timeline—a beginning, middle, and end—and characters. Unlike the authors of myths and fables, however, the honest historian attempts to record events as they actually happened without inventing the story. As we learned in the previous lesson, a narrative based on fact is called **nonfiction**, whereas **fiction** is the name for any imaginary story.

Our next story is an account of the Great Fire of Rome that relies heavily on a history written by Tacitus, a Roman senator and a student of rhetoric. Because Tacitus was only eight years old when Rome burned, he must have relied, in turn, on stories of the disaster told by older people.

After reading the story through once or twice, use one highlighter to mark facts and another highlighter in a different color to mark opinions. A **fact** is something known to be true—information based on a real or actual event. It's a fact, for example, that the Great Fire in Rome occurred in AD 64. **Opinion** is a personal claim, not necessarily based on fact. It is the author making guesses about what happened and expressing his own views.

The Great Fire in Rome, AD 64

—adapted from *The Annals* by Tacitus and *The Discovery of New Worlds* by M.B. Synge

The summer had been hot and dry. One warm night in July a fire broke out in some wooden sheds where spices, oil, and other **flammable** materials were stored. Spreading in nearby shops and fanned by the wind, the fire instantly grew and swept over the hills. All was in the wildest confusion. Men ran hither and thither. Some sought to extinguish the **conflagration**; some never heard that their houses were on fire till they lay in ashes. All shrieked and cried—men, women, children, old folks—in one vast confusion of sound. Nothing could be seen clearly in the smoke. Some stood silent and in despair. Many were engaged in rescuing their possessions, whilst others were hard at work taking **plunder**. Men quarreled over what was taken out of the burning houses, while the crush of the crowd swayed this way and that way.

As the flames engulfed the whole city, it seemed like an invader—like a Gallic army—attacking from street to street. When the fugitives stopped to glance to the rear, flames set upon them from the side or from the front. If they made their escape to a neighboring quarter, they found the flames waiting to ambush them, leaping suddenly out from buildings. Even areas that seemed far away from the danger were in the same plight.

The people no longer thought of saving goods and houses. None of them now lamented their individual losses. They all wailed over the general ruin. The treasures gained in the East, the beautiful works of the Greek artists—statues, pictures, temples—all were gone. Even the emperor's own palace fell down in a heap of ashes. A few shattered ruins stood up from among the ashes, and that was all.

The Great Fire of Rome raged for five and a half days and destroyed whole neighborhoods. When it was over the ruins smoldered balefully for many more days.

Now, Nero was not a popular emperor. Whispers that Nero had lit this fire himself grew loud. Perhaps he was angry with the Senate for refusing to let him build a bigger palace on Palatine Hill. Perhaps the fire had been started during a wild, drunken party in his gardens. Some rumors even said that while the city was burning, Nero had dressed in one of his dramatic costumes, played his lyre, and happily chanted the verses of Homer on the burning and destruction of Troy.

The emperor trembled to hear such reports. He must turn aside the guilt from himself. He must find someone else to blame. The guilt must be laid on someone like—well, the Christians, for example! Why not blame the Christians, who refused to take part in the emperor's parties and plays, his feasts and banquets? The Christians were regarded with suspicion by nearly everyone because they did not worship Roman gods. The empire would be better off with the Christians dead. When Nero announced this to the citizens, he argued that as the Christians had burned the city, they themselves should be burned. Religion was part of the unity of the Roman Empire.

Sometime later, Nero announced that a great show was to be held in the circus, within the gardens of the imperial palace. It was summertime, and the Roman people crowded in to take their places in the circus, now lit up by flaming torches. The arena was full of stakes to which were tied human beings—Christians—wrapped in linen cloths soaked in tar. While these living torches flared and the shrieks rose above the noise of the music, Nero appeared dressed in green, in an ivory chariot, and drove on the gold sand around the circus.

Lesson 8: *Historical Narrative*

Other Christians were covered with the skins of wild beasts and torn to death by dogs, or they were fastened to crosses by nails. But this was more than some of the Romans could endure, and, moved to pity, they begged that the dreadful show should cease.

"**Martyr**" is the word that people came to use to describe someone killed painfully for his or her beliefs. It comes from the Greek word, which means "witness." It is said that in this first persecution of the Christians both Paul and Peter, leaders in the growing Christian religion, suffered martyrdom. Paul, as a Roman citizen, was beheaded; Peter was reportedly crucified upside down. **A**

Tell It Back—Narration

1. Oral narration: Without looking at the historical narrative, tell the story of *The Great Fire in Rome, AD 64* as best as you remember it using your own words. Here is the opening of the story to help you get started: "The summer had been hot and dry. One warm night in July…"

2. Written narration:

   A. Write your own sentence to tell what happens at the beginning of the story.

   > Sample sentence: A huge fire breaks out in Rome and sends people running for their lives.

   _____

   B. Write your own sentence to tell what happens in the middle of the story.

   > Sample sentence: The people of Rome blame the unpopular emperor Nero for the fire.

   _____

   C. Write a sentence to tell what happens at the end of the story.

   > Sample sentence: Nero blames Christians for the fire and hideously executes them in the arena.

APaul and Peter were both leaders (apostles) of the growing Christian religion. Paul had been imprisoned in Rome for several years prior to his execution. The Romans saw religion as a unifying or divisive element in their empire. Therefore, the empire was protective of the state religion and welcomed new gods and cults only insofar as they didn't threaten the worship of Roman gods. Christians were persecuted not only because they refused to worship the Roman gods but because their numbers were growing so rapidly. At first persecutions were isolated to particular towns and cities and were sporadic. As time went on, the persecutions became more general and widespread, causing the deaths of thousands of victims.

Talk About It—

TE 1. The story seems to be divided into two parts. Who is the main character of the first part? Who is the main character of the second part? Remember that a character does not necessarily have to be a human being.

TE 2. What words and comparisons are used to make the fire seem almost human?

TE 3. Have you ever blamed someone for your mistakes? Why did you want someone else to take the blame?

TE 4. Can you think of any other examples in history when a person or a group of people became scapegoats and took the blame for another's faults?

▲ *The Scapegoat* by William Holman Hunt

Go Deeper—

1. What kind of narrative do you think *The Great Fire in Rome, AD 64* is? (See lesson 2 to see the different categories defined again.)
   a. parable
   b. myth
   c. fairy tale
   d. history

2. What is the main idea of this narrative?
   a. Don't play with matches.
   b. Bad rulers blame others for their problems.
   c. Fires can burn whole cities.
   d. One disaster always leads to another.

3. Because the fire breaks out where flammable materials are stored, "flammable" probably means:

   a. easily set on fire
   b. dangerous
   c. expensive
   d. cheap

4. The word "conflagration" indicates a specific size of a fire. The fire of Rome in AD 64 destroyed an entire city. Based on this information, see if you can number the size of the following types of fires from littlest (1) to biggest (4).

   __2__ Flame

   __1__ Spark

   __4__ Conflagration

   __3__ Blaze

5. Look up the noun "plunder" in a dictionary. Write the definition in the following space and then use it in your own complete sentence.

   Definition:

   Plunder is stolen property, usually taken by force in war.

   _____

   Sentence:

   Sample sentence: The forty thieves stashed their plunder in a secret cave.

   _____

   Why do you suppose some people would plunder houses and shops in the middle of a dangerous disaster?

   Sample answer: Some people are so greedy that they take advantage of disasters even if they jeopardize their own lives. In a disaster, they hope that no one will notice their thieving ways. They hope that other people are so distracted by terror that they won't get into trouble for doing bad things.

   _____

I thrice presented him a kingly crown,

Which he did thrice refuse. Was this ambition?

Yet Brutus says he was ambitious,

And, sure, he is an honorable man.

I speak not to disprove what Brutus spoke,

But here I am to speak what I do know.

You all did love him once, not without cause.

What cause withholds you then to mourn for him?

O judgment! Thou art fled to brutish beasts,

And men have lost their reason. Bear with me.

My heart is in the coffin there with Caesar,

And I must pause till it come back to me. (weeps)

6. Some early Christians refused to give up their faith and were martyred by the Roman emperors. The word "martyr" means:

    a. someone who commits a crime

    b. someone who dies a horrible death

    c. someone who is killed for his beliefs

    d. someone who worships God

7. Circle the adjective that best describes the emperor Nero. Find a sentence in the narrative that supports your answer and write it in the space provided.

kind   cruel

Sample answer: "While these living torches flared and the shrieks rose above the noise of the music, Nero appeared dressed in green, in an ivory chariot, and drove on the gold sand around the circus."

_____

brave   cowardly

Sample answer: "The emperor trembled to hear such reports."

_____

Writing Time—⏱

1. **DICTATION**—Your teacher will read a little part of *The Great Fire In Rome, AD 64* back to you. Please listen carefully! After your teacher reads once, she will read slowly again and include the punctuation marks. Your task will be to write down the sentences as your teacher reads them one by one.

Modify according to student level. For instance, you may want to explain or insert the dash on the board since students are likely to be unfamiliar with it.

💬 All shrieked and cried—men, women, children, old folks—in one vast confusion of sound.

💬 Whispers that Nero had lit this fire himself grew loud.

Lesson 8: Historical Narrative

_____

_____

_____

2. SENTENCE PLAY—

A. <u>As the flames engulfed the whole city, no one any longer thought of saving goods and houses.</u> In this sentence, the word "as" shows one action happening at the same time as another action. Using this sentence as a model, fill out the following sentences.

   i. As the stormy sea swallowed the whole boat, _____

        Sample sentence: As the stormy sea swallowed the whole boat, the crew was forced to swim for their lives.

  ii. As the ice cream truck drove slowly down the street, _____

        Sample sentence: As the ice cream truck drove slowly down the street, children ran after it.

 iii. As the _____, the campers quickly put up their tents.

        Sample sentence: As the storm approached, the campers quickly put up their tents.

 iv. As the _____, the Roman cavalry charged.

        Sample sentence: As the Gauls fired arrows, the Roman cavalry charged.

  v. As the _____, _____

        Sample sentence: As the knight picked up his sword, his opponent picked up a lance.

B. Challenge: This exercise is for students who are confident writers. If your students are not, please feel free to do the exercise together as a class or skip it.

Repetition is one of the most effective tools of rhetoric. Do you remember what rhetoric means?   Rhetoric is the art and practice of persuasive writing and speaking. When a word or phrase is repeated, it sinks into the listener's ears. As long as it is not used too often, repetition really makes people pay attention. I repeat: Repetition really makes people pay attention!

In our story, as the author imagines parts of the story about which he is unsure of the facts, he repeats the word "perhaps":

> Whispers that Nero had lit this fire himself grew loud. *Perhaps* he was angry with the Senate for refusing to let him build a bigger palace on Palatine Hill. *Perhaps* the fire had been started during a wild, drunken party in his gardens.

Each possible reason for the burning of the city makes Nero look worse and worse. The word "perhaps" is used as a linking word to create a short list of Nero's wickedness—he seems to have started the fire out of greed and anger, or out of drunkenness. Either way, the author clearly wants Nero to look like a terrible, selfish human being. It is astonishing to imagine a single reason that any human being would start a fire in a beloved city, but to be able to think of two or three reasons suggests, in this case, that Nero is so absent of virtue and full of vice that any number of explanations could be the case.

Use the word "perhaps" at the start of the following sentences to take guesses about the two people described.

i.   Lilia really enjoyed visiting the zoo. (Make Lilia seem like an intelligent girl.)

Perhaps she ___ Sample sentence: Perhaps she liked watching the playful monkeys. _____

_____.

Perhaps ___ Sample sentence: Perhaps she studied the habits of the zebras. _____

_____.

ii. Lilia really enjoyed visiting the zoo. (Now make Lilia seem like a foolish girl.)

Perhaps she ___ Sample sentence: Perhaps she liked swimming with the crocodiles. _____

_____.

Perhaps ___ Sample sentence: Perhaps playing tag with a wild boar was her favorite part. _

_____.

iii. Rodrigo's favorite sport was soccer. (Make Rodrigo look like a great soccer player.)

Perhaps he _ Sample sentence: Perhaps he enjoyed stealing the ball from the other team.

_____.

Perhaps _ Sample sentence: Perhaps he liked to score goals against a tough defense. _____

_____.

iv. Rodrigo's favorite sport was soccer. (Make Rodrigo look like a foolish soccer player.)

Perhaps he _ Sample sentence: Perhaps he enjoyed dancing in front of the goalie. _____

_____.

Perhaps _ Sample sentence: Perhaps he liked doing cartwheels across the field. _____

_____.

3. **COPIOUSNESS**—In the last lesson, your copiousness focused on adjectives. This time you'll focus on nouns. As you already know, a noun is a person, place, thing, or idea, such as "cup," "Pennsylvania," "soccer ball," or "love."

When you look at this picture to the left, what do you see? Did you answer "dog," which is a general name for this type of animal, or did you answer "Poodle"?

When you look at this picture to the right, what do you see? Did you answer "human being," or did you say something more specific like "Roman soldier"?

Almost always, the more specific you are with nouns, the more interesting your writing will be.

A. Choose more specific nouns for the words underlined in the following sentences and rewrite the complete sentences.

Example: Every <u>day</u>, I drink <u>a hot drink</u> and eat a bowl of <u>cereal</u>.

Change to: Every morning, I drink hot coffee and eat a bowl of granola.

i. Snapping and snarling, a <u>dog</u> chased a <u>cat</u> up a <u>tree</u>.

Sample sentence: Snapping and snarling, a terrier chased a tabby up a fence post.

ii. The sun went down over <u>the city</u> as lights began to twinkle in <u>the buildings</u>.

Sample sentence: The sun went down over New Orleans as lights began to twinkle in the skyscrapers.

iii. The <u>man and woman</u> drove off in a <u>vehicle</u> to enjoy <u>the holiday</u> at <u>a place</u>.

Sample sentence: The husband and wife drove off in a van to enjoy Memorial Day at Rehoboth Beach.

iv. The naughty <u>little kids</u> hid a <u>reptile</u> in my lunch <u>container</u>.

Sample sentence: The naughty girls hid a boa constrictor in my metal lunch tin.

v. Let's meet at <u>a restaurant</u> for <u>food</u> and <u>drink</u>.

Sample sentence: Let's meet at Steak & Shake for burgers and cola.

B. Replace the underlined noun phrase with a single, specific noun. Often a single, specific word is more direct and vivid than several words.

Example: <u>The soccer player</u> caught the soccer ball.

Change to: The goalie caught the soccer ball.

i.   <u>The ball of flaming gas</u> sits at the center of our solar system.

Sample sentence: The sun sits at the center of our solar system.

_____

_____

ii.   <u>The royal ruler</u> is in charge of this kingdom.

Sample sentence: The queen is in charge of this kingdom.

_____

_____

iii. George is <u>a mean kid</u> who is always picking on little kids.

Sample sentence: George is a bully who is always picking on little kids.

_____

iv. The robin yanked a <u>soft, squirming creature</u> from the grass.

Sample sentence: The robin yanked a worm from the grass.

_____

v. Of all the instruments in the orchestra, my favorite is <u>a stringed instrument</u>.

Sample sentence: Of all the instruments in the orchestra, my favorite is the cello.

_____

C. Change the underlined noun in each sentence into a noun phrase that is more descriptive than a single word. A noun phrase can include an article (a, an, the), adjectives, and sometimes a preposition, as well as a noun.

Example: The <u>lion</u> roars as the sun sets over the grasslands.
Change to: The king of beasts roars as the sun sets over the grasslands.

Example: It took a month for the expedition to climb the <u>mountain</u>.
Change to: It took a month for the expedition to climb the giant tower of rock.

i. Eagerly we warmed our numb fingers over the <u>fire</u>.

Sample sentence: Eagerly we warmed our numb fingers over the leaping flames.

_____

ii. The <u>snow</u> blew wildly across the plains.

Sample sentence: The crystals of ice blew wildly across the plains.

_____

iii. On the back of her <u>horse</u>, the rider saw the brush fence ahead.

Sample sentence: On the back of her brave steed, the rider saw the brush fence ahead.

_____

iv. The stagecoach was stopped in the desert by <u>robbers</u>.

Sample sentence: The stagecoach was stopped in the desert by a gang of bandits.

_____

v. Please put <u>meat</u> on the grill for me.

Sample sentence: Please put another sirloin steak on the grill for me.

_____

Lesson 8: Historical Narrative

4. **SUMMARY**—When you summarize a story, you want to keep only the most important ideas. The rest of the writing can be done away with.

   A. Read *The Great Fire in Rome, AD 64* again. Decide which ideas are the most important and circle them.

   B. Underline any specific words that are essential to telling the story. Use these words to tell the story briefly in your summary.**ᴮ**

   C. Rewrite the historical narrative in exactly six sentences.

> **ᴮ**We are having students transition to underlining content that should be included in their summaries rather than crossing out content that should be excluded. However, strikeouts are indicated in the teacher's edition for your ease of use.

The Great Fire in Rome, AD 64

—adapted from The Annals *by Tacitus and* The Discovery of New Worlds *by M.B. Synge*

~~The summer had been hot and dry.~~ One warm night in July a fire broke out in some wooden sheds ~~where spices, oil, and other flammable materials were stored. Spreading in nearby shops and fanned by the wind,~~ the fire instantly grew and swept over the hills. ~~All was in the wildest confusion. Men ran hither and thither. Some sought to extinguish the conflagration; some never heard that their houses were on fire till they lay in ashes. All shrieked and cried—men, women, children, old folks—in one vast confusion of sound. Nothing could be seen clearly in the smoke. Some stood silent and in despair. Many were engaged in rescuing their possessions, whilst others were hard at work taking plunder. Men quarreled over what was taken out of the burning houses, while the crush of the crowd swayed this way and that way.~~

~~As the flames engulfed the whole city,~~ it seemed like an <u>invader</u>—like a Gallic army —attacking from street to street. When the fugitives stopped to glance to the rear, flames set upon them from the side or from the front. If they made their escape to a neighboring quarter, they found the flames waiting to ambush them, leaping suddenly out from buildings. Even areas that seemed far away from the danger were in the same plight.

The people no longer thought of saving goods and houses. None of them now lamented their individual losses. They all wailed over the general ruin. The treasures gained in the East, the beautiful works of the Greek artists—statues, pictures, temples—all were gone. Even the emperor's own palace fell down in a heap of ashes. A few shattered ruins stood up from among the ashes, and that was all.

The Great Fire of Rome raged for five and a half days and destroyed whole neighborhoods. ~~When it was over~~ the ruins smoldered balefully for many more days.

Now, Nero was not a popular emperor. ~~Whispers that Nero had lit this fire himself grew loud.~~ Perhaps he was angry with the Senate for refusing to let him build a bigger palace on Palatine Hill. Perhaps the fire had been started during a wild, drunken party in his gardens. Some rumors even said that while the city was burning, Nero had dressed in one of his dramatic costumes, played his lyre, and happily chanted the verses of Homer on the burning and destruction of Troy.

The emperor trembled to hear such reports. ~~He must turn aside the guilt from himself.~~ He must find someone else to blame. The guilt must be laid on someone like—well, the Christians, for example! ~~Why not blame the Christians, who refused to~~ take part in the emperor's parties and plays, his feasts and banquets? The Christians were regarded with suspicion by nearly everyone because they did not ~~worship Roman gods~~. The empire would be better off with the Christians dead. When Nero announced this to the citizens, he argued that as the Christians had burned the city, they themselves should be burned. Religion was part of the unity of the Roman Empire.

Sometime later, Nero announced that a great show was to be held in the circus, within the gardens of the imperial palace. It was summertime, and the Roman people crowded in to take their places in the circus, now lit up by flaming torches. ~~The arena was full of stakes to which were tied human beings—Christians—~~ wrapped in linen cloths soaked in tar. While these living torches flared and the shrieks rose above the noise of the music, Nero appeared dressed in green, in an ivory chariot, and drove on the gold sand around the circus.

Other Christians were covered with the skins of wild beasts and ~~torn to death by dogs,~~ or they were fastened to crosses by nails. But this was more than some of the Romans could endure, and, moved to <u>pity</u>, they begged that the dreadful show should cease.

Lesson 8: Historical Narrative

~~"Martyr" is the word that people came to use to describe someone killed painfully for his or her beliefs. It comes from the Greek word, which means "witness." It is said that in this first persecution of the Christians both Paul and Peter, leaders in the growing Christian religion, suffered martyrdom. Paul, as a Roman citizen, was beheaded; Peter was reportedly crucified upside down.~~

Summary: _____

Sample summary:
One warm night in July, a fire broke out in Rome. It grew and swept over the city, destroying houses and treasures like a terrible invader. After it was over, the people whispered that the fire had been set by the emperor Nero. In order to turn the guilt aside from himself, Nero blamed the Christians, who did not worship the Roman gods. He had them set on fire in the circus like human torches, while others were torn to death by dogs. But this was more than some of the Romans could endure, and, moved to pity, they begged that the dreadful show of martyrs should cease.

5. **FACT AND OPINION**—Did the Roman emperor Nero really cause the fire of Rome? We may never know for sure, but we do know that he took advantage of the burned-down city to build himself a huge palace. After the fire cleared away the old buildings on Palatine Hill, he started building the famous palace *Domus Aurea*, or Golden House.

Now read the following passage, which involves aspects of the same story but comes from a different source, the Roman historian Suetonius and the writer H.A. Guerber. Highlight the parts that seem to be factual with one color and the parts that seem to be based on opinion with another color.

fact

opinion

The Golden House

—adapted, in part, from H.A. Guerber's *The Story of the Romans* and from *The Twelve Caesars* by Suetonius

As Rome had been partly destroyed by the fire, Nero now began to rebuild it with great magnificence. He also built a palace for his own use, which was known as the Golden House, because it glittered without and within with this precious metal. Some people said he deliberately set the fire so that he would have room to build the magnificent palace.

Nero surrounded it with pastures for sheep, groves of trees, and an artificial lake. It was "a countryside in the city." In the entrance hall, he had his artists raise a bronze statue of himself, the *Colossus of Nero*, which stood at 120 feet tall. The main dining room was circular, and its roof, painted with the sun and the stars, revolved slowly, day and night, in time with the sky. Seawater, or sulfur water, was always on tap in the baths.

Most likely the Golden Palace was built only for parties and pleasure. It contained as many as 300 rooms, but not a single bedroom. Once it was completed, Nero supposedly said, "Good! At last I can live like a human being." Nero slept in his other palace on Quirinal Hill.

Nero was guilty of many follies, such as worshiping a favorite monkey, fishing with a golden net, and spending large sums in gifts to undeserving courtiers. He is said never to have worn the same garment twice.

Of course, so cruel and capricious a ruler as Nero could not be loved, and you will not be surprised to hear that many Romans found his rule unbearable and formed a conspiracy to kill him.

6. **AMPLIFICATION**—Challenge: Here is a brief eyewitness account of another Roman disaster, the destruction of Pompeii. Pompeii was a prosperous port city filled with holiday villas, fancy inns, large markets, and luxurious hot baths. The artwork of Pompeii, uncovered by excavations, includes spectacular statues, mosaics, and paintings. The city of about 18,000 was wiped off the map by the eruption of Mount Vesuvius, a volcano near Naples, Italy, in AD 79. [c]

[c] Please be aware that this describes a natural disaster that could be upsetting to some children.

The Destruction of Pompeii, AD 79

—adapted from a letter by Pliny the Younger

On the first day a cloud in the form of a very tall trunk ascended into the sky over Mount Vesuvius like a pine tree shot up to a great height. It spread itself out at the top into what looked like branches. Then at night, broad flames shone out in several places from the volcano, which the darkness made still brighter and clearer.

The next day my uncle and his friends consulted together whether it was safe to trust to the houses, which rocked from side to side with frequent and violent earthquakes, or whether we should fly to the open fields, where the stones and cinders fell in large showers.

Even though the sun was up, the sky was blacker than the deepest night. The courtyard of the apartment began filling with ashes, and it wouldn't be long before the whole house was covered.

My uncle called for some cold water, which he drank, when immediately the flames, preceded by a strong whiff of sulfur, dispersed the rest of the party and obliged him to rise. He raised himself up with the assistance of two of his servants and instantly fell down dead, suffocated by some gross and noxious vapor.

We took to the road, but we were afraid of being crushed in the dark by the crowds following us. The ashes fell thick upon us. You could hear the shrieks of women, the screams of children, and the shouts of men. Some were calling for their children, others for their parents, others for their husbands, seeking to recognize each other by the voices that replied. We had to keep shaking ashes off of our tunics, otherwise we should have been crushed and buried in the heap. Every object that presented itself to our eyes (which were extremely weakened) seemed changed, being covered deep with ashes as if with snow.

Your job is to amplify one of the paragraphs above. Add details that appeal to the senses: sight, sound, smell, taste, and touch. Invent dialogue for the family consultation or for the crowd in the dark. Ask yourself what you would be thinking and feeling if you were the eyewitness, Pliny the Younger, and try to capture your emotions. Use a separate piece of paper if necessary.

> Sample amplification:
> Paragraph #3 amplified:
> Even though the sun was up, the sky was blacker than the deepest night. We stretched our hands before us and saw nothing—it was as though we had become bodiless ghosts. Ashes poured upon our villa as thick as a plague of locusts. If we waited any longer, we would be buried in the house and the house, in turn, would be buried like a coffin. "Run, run!" I yelled, coughing and coughing. We groped for the door handle and pushed our way into the street. We saw the flashing glow of Vesuvius high in the pitchy sky and then we ran— we ran through ashes that were ankle deep.

_____

_____

_____

_____

Lesson 8: Historical Narrative

_____

_____

_____

_____

_____

_____

_____

Speak It— 🎙️

Your teacher will divide the class into partnerships of two. First, each student will write an introduction for his partner by inventing the information found in the following list.

- Name of the speaker: Choose a Roman name such as Amicus, Agrippa, Antonius, Benedictus, or Brutus for boys or Amica, Agrippina, Antonia, Aurora, Benedicta, or Britannia for girls.

- Occupation of the speaker: Choose a Roman job, such as a senator, a farmer, a soldier, a teacher, a merchant, a sculptor, or a lawyer.

- Date that the speaker was in Pompeii: August 24, AD 79.

- What the speaker was doing in Pompeii: selling olive oil, creating a mosaic, fighting pirates, farming wheat, picking grapes, vacationing in her villa, and so on.

- Why the speaker should be listened to: She is an eyewitness after all!

One student will read his fictional introduction of the "main speaker," sharing details such as the speaker's name, occupation, and so forth. Following the introduction, the other student, who is playing the part of "main speaker," will dramatically read her amplification of *The Destruction of Pompeii, AD 79* from a podium.

Keep in mind that an introduction sets the stage for the main speaker. It should help the audience eagerly anticipate the speech.

Lesson 8: Historical Narrative

Talk About It—

1. The fire is the main character of the first part. The main character of the second part is the emperor Nero.

2. The fire takes on the human qualities of an invader by attacking and ambushing people. This is an example of anthropomorphism, a concept introduced in *Writing & Rhetoric: Fable*.

3. People often blame someone else to escape punishment.

   If it's true that Nero helped to start the great fire, he made a scapegoat of the Christians to escape the anger of his people. The person or object blamed for the faults of another is called a scapegoat. This term comes from a practice of the ancient Hebrews during a holiday known as Yom Kippur, or the Day of Atonement. On this day, the high priest symbolically laid the sins, or the bad deeds, of the people on the head of a goat. Then the goat was driven into the desert wilderness surrounding their camp. The suggestion was that the goat would take the burden of those deeds. In the same way, the Christians were made to take the burden of responsibility for the fire; they were made scapegoats by Nero.

4. If he did not torch his city, then unpopular Nero was himself a scapegoat of the Roman people. Marie Antoinette was blamed for the problems of France and was beheaded during the French Revolution. In more recent history, Jews were blamed by the Nazi regime for Germany's problems, and approximately six million of them were killed. Even more recently, terrorists blame the United States for problems in their own lands and kill innocent people to get attention.

Notes

The purpose of this lesson is to introduce "who," "what," "when," "where," "why," and "how" as aids to writing any narrative, but especially a historical narrative.

In this lesson, your students will practice:
- critical thinking
- using the five *W*s to better understand historical fiction
- strengthening weak verb choices
- summarizing historical narrative

Lesson 9 ·

The Five Ws

"Who," "what," "when," "where," and "why" . . . These are the questions any person must ask in order to write a historical narrative. "Who," "what," "when," "where," and "why". . . The five *W*s! These are the questions a reporter must ask in order to write a story for a newspaper or a storyteller must ask in order to weave a tale of fiction.

Rudyard Kipling, English novelist and poet, wrote this little rhyme about the five *W*s:

> I keep six honest serving-men
>
> (They taught me all I knew);
>
> Their names are What and Why and When
>
> And How and Where and Who.

As you can see, Kipling—and many others—adds "how" to the list. The five *W*s (and one *H*) have been an important part of teaching rhetoric for centuries. They can be found in the words of Hermagoras of Temnos, a Greek rhetorician who taught in Rome, from the first century BC.

> *Quis, quid, quando, ubi, cur, quem ad modum, quibus adminiculis.*
>
> (Who, what, when, where, why, how, in what way, by what means.)

Let's get some practice with this idea. After you read the following narrative, *Zenobia, Queen of Palmyra*, you will be asked to find the five *W*s and one *H*.

134

Zenobia, Queen of Palmyra

—adapted from *Historic Girls* by E.S. Brooks and
The Story of the Romans by H.A. Guerber

Many miles and many days' journey toward the rising sun, over seas and mountains and deserts—farther to the east than Rome or Constantinople or even Jerusalem and old Damascus—stand the ruins of a once mighty city. It is known as Palmyra, once one of the most beautiful cities in the world.

Nature and art combined to make it glorious. Like a glittering **mirage** out of the sand-swept desert arose its palaces and temples and grandly sculptured archways. It had aqueducts and monuments and gleaming porticos with countless groves of palm trees and gardens full of flowers. It had wells and fountains, market and circus, and broad streets stretching away to the city gates and lined on either side with magnificent colonnades of rose-colored marble. Such was Palmyra in the year 250.[A]

[A] Zenobia was born circa AD 240 and died sometime after AD 274. This story indicates that she was twelve years old in the year AD 250, which is more or less accurate.

A boy of sixteen and a girl of twelve looked down from a balcony upon the beautiful Street of the Thousand Columns. Both were handsome and healthy. The boy was named Odaenathus and the girl was Zenobia. As they looked lazily on the crowds below, a sudden exclamation from the lad caused his companion to raise her flashing black eyes inquiringly to his face. "What troubles you, my Odaenathus?" she asked.

"There, there! Look there, Zenobia!" replied the boy excitedly. "Coming through the Damascus arch, the Romans have returned. We thought them to be in Emesa."

The girl's glance followed his guiding finger. She saw the bright April sun gleam down upon the standard of Rome, with its eagle crest and its S.P.Q.R. **B** design beneath. There came a trumpet peal, and, swinging into the great Street of the Thousand Columns at the head of his light-armed legionaries, rode the centurion Rufinus.

"But why should the coming of the Roman so trouble you, my Odaenathus?" she asked. "We are neither Jew nor Christian that we should fear his **wrath**, but free Palmyreans who bend the knee neither to Roman nor Persian masters."

"Who will bend the knee no longer, be it ever so little, my cousin," exclaimed the lad hotly. "Yet see—who comes now?" he cried. At once the attention of the young people was turned in the opposite direction as they saw, streaming out of the great fortress-like courtyard of the Temple of the Sun, another hurrying crowd, the glint of weaponry in their hands.

Then young Odaenathus gave a cry of joy. "See, Zenobia; they come, they come!" he cried. "It is my father, Odaenathus, the chief of the lords of Palmyra. This day will we fling off the Roman **yoke** and become the true and unconquered lords of Palmyra. And I, too, must join them," he added.

But the young girl detained him. "Wait, cousin," she said. "Watch and wait. Your father will scarce attempt so brave a deed today, with these new Roman soldiers in our gates. Truly that isn't wise."

The boy broke out again. "They have seen each other," he said. "Both sides are pressing on!"

"Yes, and they will meet under this very balcony," said Zenobia.

Moved both by interest and desire, the dark-eyed Syrian girl, to

Lesson 9: The Five Ws

whom fear was never known, looked down upon the tossing sea of spears and lances and glittering shields and helmets that swayed and **surged** in the street below.

"So, Odaenathus!" said Rufinus, the tribune, reining in his horse and speaking in harsh and commanding tones. "Why do you greet me with all these armed followers?"

"Are my movements of such importance to the noble tribune that he must question a free leader of Palmyra as to the number and manner of his servants?" asked Odaenathus haughtily.

"Dog of a Palmyrean! Slave of a camel-driver!" said the Roman angrily. "Free, never! None are free but Romans."

"Have a care, O Rufinus," said the older Odaenathus boldly. "Choose wiser words if you would have peaceful ways. Palmyra will not tolerate any such **slander** of her foremost men."

"And Rome will not tolerate such men as you, traitor," said Rufinus. "Ay, traitor, I say," he repeated. "Strike!" At his word the short sword in the ready hand of the big foot soldier went straight into Odaenathus's chest. The chief of Palmyra fell dead in the street.

So sudden and so unexpected was the blow that the Palmyreans stood as if stunned, unable to comprehend what had happened. But the Roman was swift to act.

"Sound, trumpets! Down, pikes!" he cried, and as the trumpet peal rose loud and clear, fresh soldiers came hurrying through the gate.

Before the lowered pikes could fully disperse the crowd, the throng parted and through the swaying mob there burst a **lithe** and flying figure—a brown-skinned maid of twelve with streaming hair, loose robe, and angry, flashing eyes. Right under the lowered pikes she darted and, flushed and panting, she defiantly faced the astonished Rufinus. Close behind her came an equally excited lad who, when he saw the stricken body of his father on the marble street, flung himself weeping upon it.

Zenobia's eyes flashed still more angrily. "Assassin, murderer!" she cried. "You have slain my kinsman and Odaenathus's father. How dare you? How dare you!" she repeated vehemently, and then, flushing with deeper scorn, she added, "Roman, I hate you! Would that I were a man. Then should all Palmyra know how—"

B S.P.Q.R. are initials that spell out *Senatus Populusque Romanus*, which means "The Senate and People of Rome." It became a symbol of the Roman Republic and then the Roman Empire.

"Whip these children home," broke in the stern Rufinus, "or fetch them by the ears to their nurses and their toys."

The struggling children were half led, half carried into the sculptured **atrium** of the palace of Odaenathus. There under the vines and bowers of the garden, young Odaenathus and Zenobia swore eternal hatred for Rome.

Not long after, the kingdom of Palmyra gained in power and extent. The young Odaenathus became ruler and a strong war leader. He set about flexing the muscles of Palmyra by conquering Persia in the name of the Romans. Odaenathus then married Zenobia, and they had two children together. It seemed that they should have lived happily ever after, except that Zenobia still secretly hated bowing to Rome. Her husband warned her, "We have prospered under Rome. Let us forget our childish oath."

But then the young Odaenathus was also murdered by an assassin, and so Zenobia, his wife, governed in the name of her young son. The young girl had grown into a beautiful and very able queen. She wished to rival Cleopatra in magnificence of attire and pomp, as well as in beauty.

Never tame in spirit, Zenobia took the title Empress of the East and tried to drive the Romans out of Asia forever. In full armor, she led her troops into battle and conquered Egypt. She also entered into an **alliance** with the Persians. With the back of her kingdom secure, she set her sights on Asia Minor.

Meanwhile, Aurelian, the emperor of Rome, was forced to subdue the Goths [c] before he could lead his legions against Zenobia. Eventually he marched the power and might of Rome against Palmyra. The queen of Palmyra was then defeated and her capital taken. Though she attempted to flee, she fell into the hands of the Romans. Many of Zenobia's most faithful supporters were killed.

Palmyra itself was at first spared, but the inhabitants revolted soon after the Romans had left. Aurelian therefore retraced his steps, took the city for the second time, and, after killing nearly all the people, destroyed both houses and walls. Its wealth was so great that even the Romans were dazzled by the amount of gold they saw in Aurelian's triumph.

They also stared in wonder at Zenobia, the proud eastern queen, who was forced to walk in front of Aurelian's chariot. The unhappy woman could scarcely carry the weight of the priceless jewels she was forced to wear for the occasion.

Lesson 9: The Five Ws

When the triumph was over, Zenobia was allowed to live in peace and great comfort in a palace near Tibur, and there she brought up her children as if she had been only a Roman mother. Her daughters married Roman nobles, and one of her sons was given a small kingdom by the generous Aurelian.

Tell It Back—**Narration**

1. Without looking at the story, tell back *Zenobia, Queen of Palmyra* as best as you can remember it using your own words and any words from the story. For further practice, you could record your telling back and play it afterward. Remember to keep the events of the story in their proper order.

Here are the first sentences to get you started:

Many miles and many days' journey toward the rising sun, over seas and mountains and deserts—farther to the east than Rome or Constantinople or even Jerusalem and old Damascus—stand the ruins of a once mighty city. It is known as Palmyra, once one of the most beautiful cities in the world.

2. Put the events in proper order by numbering them from 1–6.

____2____ Rufinus the centurion rides into the city with his Roman soldiers.

____4____ Zenobia and Odaenathus swear eternal hatred to Rome.

____3____ Rufinus and the chief of Palmyra quarrel. The chief is killed.

____6____ Zenobia is defeated and led captive down the streets of Rome.

____5____ Queen Zenobia revolts against Rome and goes to war.

____1____ Young Odaenathus and young Zenobia are looking at the city of Palmyra from a balcony.

c The Goths were a warlike German tribe that inhabited the forests north of Rome.

Talk About It—

TE 1. Of the five *Ws*, which question do you ask the most? Which question is often the hardest to answer?

TE 2. Why do you suppose people fight for a position such as emperor of Rome or queen of Palmyra? What do they hope to gain? What are some of the negatives of such a powerful position? Why is the character of a ruler important to the people of a kingdom?

TE 3. Examine the painting *Queen Zenobia's Last Look Upon Palmyra* by Herbert Schmaltz. This painting shows the queen as she is about to be led away to Rome as a prisoner of Emperor Aurelian. What do you think the queen is thinking as she stands above her city in chains?

▲ *Queen Zenobia's Last Look Upon Palmyra* by Herbert Schmaltz

Go Deeper—

Circle or supply the correct answer(s):

1. Choose the best title for this story from the following options:
   a. The Revenge of Rufinus
   b. The Revenge of Zenobia
   c. The Rise and Fall of Zenobia
   d. The Sorrow of Young Odaenathus

2. Who is the protagonist of the narrative?
   a. Zenobia
   b. Rufinus
   c. Odaenathus
   d. Aurelian

3. Who are the two antagonists of the narrative?

   a. Zenobia

   b. Rufinus

   c. Odaenathus

   d. Aurelian

4. What is Zenobia's goal? Answer in one sentence.

   Sample sentence: Zenobia's goal is to free Palmyra from the Romans.

   _____

   _____

5. What stands in the way of Zenobia's goal? In other words, what is the source of conflict?

   Sample answer: The Roman army and Roman leaders stand in the way of Zenobia's goal.

   _____

   _____

6. Choose one of the bolded words in the narrative of Zenobia. Look up the word in a dictionary. Write the definition in the space provided and then use it in your own complete sentence.

   Definition:

   _____

   _____

   _____

   Sentence:

   Answers will vary. The following are some sample sentences using words from the story:
   - My parents made an alliance when they got married to each other.
   - Wrath is stronger than anger and makes me scared just hearing the word.
   - When a group of people surge forward others often get trampled and injured.
   - Oxen wear a yoke to plow the field side by side, but a yoke is also used to speak of anything that binds us to another.

   Have students share their vocabulary words with their classmates so that all of these delightful, but difficult, words can be known. Definitions can also be found in the glossary.

7. Use a thesaurus to look up the word you chose in the previous exercise. Write down other words that are synonyms. A synonym is a word that has nearly the same meaning.

> Alliance: association, coalition, relationship, grouping, union, pact
> Surged: rushed, flowed, poured, gushed, coursed, heaved
> Yoke: oppression, burden, bondage, encumbrance, load
> Wrath: anger, rage, fury, ire, madness

8. Use two sentences to answer each of the following journalistic questions. The first sentence should mirror the question, and the second sentence should explain or add to the answer. Here's an example for you:

Who is the main character of *Zenobia, Queen of Palmyra*?
Sample answer: Zenobia is the main character. She was the queen of Palmyra, a city in the deserts of Syria.

a. *What* is the main event or action of the narrative?

> Answers will vary. Students could consider the main action to be the murder of the older Odaenathus, the moment when Zenobia comes to hate Rome and desires to lead a rebellion, Zenobia's battle with Rome, or her eventual capture.
> Sample answer: The main action is Zenobia's oath of eternal hatred toward Rome. She leads a rebellion that succeeds in capturing Egypt and parts of Asia Minor.

b. *When* does the narrative take place?

> Sample answer: The narrative takes place in the ancient world. The year is 250.

c. *Where* does the narrative take place?

> Sample answer: The narrative mostly takes place in Palmyra. This ancient city was located near the Syrian desert.

Lesson 9: The Five W's

d. *How* does the antagonist succeed in overcoming the protagonist?

> Sample answer: Aurelian succeeds in overcoming Zenobia because Roman armies are
> stronger. He shows off his victory by parading Zenobia down the streets of Rome.

e. *Why* do think the author has written this narrative? What was his purpose? What is he trying to say about Zenobia?

> Sample answer: The author has written this narrative to show how courageous Zenobia
> was. He could have portrayed her as a power-hungry woman, but instead he chose to
> show her as a freedom-loving Palmyrean.

Writing Time— 🕐

1. **DICTATION**—Your teacher will read a little part of *Zenobia, Queen of Palmyra* back to you. Please listen carefully! After your teacher reads once, she will read slowly again and include the punctuation marks. Your task will be to write down the sentences as your teacher reads them one by one.

> Modify according to student level. Be sure to spell difficult words on the board before
> you get started.
>
> 💬 Many miles and many days' journey toward the rising sun, over seas and mountains and deserts, stand the ruins of a once mighty city.
>
> 💬 But the young girl detained him. "Wait, cousin," she said. "Watch and wait. Your father will scarce attempt so brave a deed today."

2. SENTENCE PLAY—

A. "Though" and "although" are two words that change the outcome of a sentence. Take a look at the following sentence: "Though his soldiers were outnumbered, Constantine won the day." If someone's soldiers are outnumbered, we expect them to be defeated. The use of "though" or "although" changes what we expect to happen. What actually happens is something different than defeat—Constantine wins the day. Here are some additional examples:

"Though he was dressed like a clown, he made the audience cry." We expect a clown to be funny. This clown was not!

"Though I walk through the valley of the shadow of death, I will fear no evil" (Psalm 23:4). We expect David would have been scared in the shadow of death, but he wasn't.

"Although light passes through dirty windows, it is not polluted" (adapted from the writings of Augustine of Hippo). We expect anything that passes through dirt to become dirty, but light alone stays pure.

Using these "though" and "although" sentences as models, complete the following sentences.

i. Although the cake looked delicious, _____

    Sample sentence: Although the cake looked delicious, it tasted like rotten eggs.

ii. Though the water was chilly, _____

    Sample sentence: Though the water was chilly, we still went swimming.

iii. Although _____ Sample sentence: Although the dancer stepped on her feet, the queen still smiled graciously.

_____, the queen still smiled graciously.

                              Lesson 9: *The Five Ws*

iv. Though ___ [Sample sentence: Though I fell off the horse, I dusted off my jeans and climbed back into the saddle.] ___

_____, I

dusted off my jeans and climbed back into the saddle.

v. Though ___ [Sample sentence: Though I lost my key, I managed to pick the lock.] ___

_____, _____

_____.

B. *Many miles and many days' journey toward the rising sun, over seas and moun-tains and deserts, stand the ruins of a once mighty city.* This long sentence takes us on an interesting journey across the world. Let's write three new sentences that also take us on a journey.

i. Say you're heading from your bedroom to the kitchen. What obstacles might you have to cross?

Many inches and many centimeters' journey toward the kitchen, over

___ [Sample sentence: Many inches and many centimeters' journey toward the kitchen, over dirty socks and carpets and our pet cat, stands my refrigerator.] and _____

and _____, stands my refrigerator.

ii. Now take us on a long journey to the home of grandparents or family friends.

Many _____ [Sample sentence: Many hours and many long miles' journey toward the south, over bridges and highways and country roads, lives my grandmother in Florida.]

and many _____s' journey

toward the _____ ,

                    a direction would fit here

over _____

and _____

and _____,

lives my _____.

iii. Using these sentences as models, create your own journey sentence. The journey could be across your school, park, pool, city, or state.

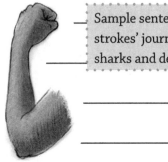

Sample sentence: Many backstrokes and many long side strokes' journey toward the setting sun, over coral reefs and sharks and deep sea valleys, sits the happy island of Maui.

_____

_____

3. **COPIOUSNESS**—Just as you should use specific and interesting nouns and adjectives, you should also express yourself with strong verbs. A verb is the action word of a sentence or the word that shows a state of being.

For example:

Miguel <u>kicked</u> the soccer ball. "Kicked" is an action verb.

Miguel <u>is</u> a soccer player. "Is" is a verb that describes a state of being.

Verbs also tell us whether the action happened in the present, past, or future. This time aspect of a verb is called its tense.

Present: Michele <u>rides</u> her bike. Michele <u>is</u> a cyclist.
Past: Michele <u>rode</u> her bike. Michele <u>was</u> a cyclist.
Future: Michele <u>will ride</u> her bike. Michele <u>will be</u> a cyclist.

Grammar isn't always simple to explain. There are a number of other tenses, but let's not worry about them yet.

A. Find synonyms that are more specific and interesting for the following action verbs. Keep the tense (past, present, future) that the first sentence uses. Notice in the examples that one sentence happens in the present ("look") and one in the past ("found").

Example: Stamp collectors <u>look</u> for the rare Inverted Jenny stamp.
Change to: Stamp collectors hunt for the rare Inverted Jenny stamp.

Lesson 9: The Five W's

Example: Archaeologists <u>found</u> the treasures of Tutankhamun.

Change to: Archaeologists unearthed the treasures of Tutankhamun.

i. The mother proudly <u>smiled</u> during her son's wedding.

Sample sentence: The mother proudly grinned/beamed during her son's wedding.

ii. She <u>wrote</u> her name at the bottom of the check.

Sample sentence: She signed/scribbled her name at the bottom of the check.

iii. Because of the rain, they <u>kept themselves</u> at home.

Sample sentence: Because of the rain, they remained/stayed/lingered at home.

iv. The player <u>played with</u> the basketball.

Sample sentence: The player dribbled/scooped/dunked the basketball.

v. The zookeeper lovingly <u>touches</u> the panda bear.

Sample sentence: The zookeeper lovingly pets/pats/scratches the panda bear.

B. Change the state-of-being verbs into action verbs in the following sentences. You may alter the sentence if you wish as long as the meaning and the verb tense remains the same.

Example: Jerry <u>was</u> a bullfrog.

Change to: Jerry died a bullfrog.

Example: In her opinion, punk rock <u>is</u> awful.

Change to: In her opinion, punk rock sounds awful.

i. The shrimp cocktail <u>was</u> delicious.

Sample sentence: The shrimp cocktail tasted delicious.

ii. Against their bare skin, the seawater <u>is</u> refreshing.

Sample sentence: Against their bare skin, the seawater feels refreshing.

iii. After winning the tournament, she felt as though she <u>was</u> on a cloud.

Sample sentence: After winning the tournament, she felt as though she floated on a cloud.

iv. They <u>are</u> like angels when they dance.

Sample sentence: They twirl like angels when they dance.

v. Covered in cow dung, the shoe <u>was</u> disgusting.

Sample sentence: Covered in cow dung, the shoe smelled disgusting.

Action verbs have two voices: **active voice** and **passive voice**. In the active voice, the subject is doing the action of the verb: *The bear **rides** the bicycle.* In the passive voice, the subject is being acted upon by the verb instead of the other way around: *The bicycle **was ridden** by the bear.* The active voice is almost always best because the subject is doing the action of the verb. Sentences that use the active voice get to the point faster; the passive voice often requires the use of more words. The passive voice uses weak verbs (such as is, am, are, was, were, be, being, been); the active voice uses stronger verbs. The passive voice can be confusing or unclear because it often doesn't identify who is performing the action of the situation. The passive voice can also lead to awkward writing. Most passive-voice sentences use the connecting word "by": The cake was baked *by* Jenny. The jet is flown *by* the pilot.

The following sentences are written in the **passive voice**. Change them to make them more active and interesting.

Example: The picture was painted by Van Gogh.
Change to: Van Gogh painted the picture.

Example: All men are endowed by their Creator with certain unalienable rights.
Change to: The Creator endowed all men with certain unalienable rights.

i. The balls were dropped by the juggler.

   Sample sentence: The juggler dropped the balls.

ii. The cut is being stitched up by the nurse.

   Sample sentence: The nurse stitches up the cut.

iii. Alexander the Great was carried into battle by his horse, Bucephalus.

   Sample sentence: The horse Bucephalus carried Alexander the Great into battle.

iv. Queen Elizabeth was called Good Queen Bess by her subjects.

   Sample sentence: Her subjects called Queen Elizabeth Good Queen Bess.

v. Around the world, gold is panned for by prospectors.

   Sample sentence: Around the world, prospectors pan for gold.

vi. The twelve red roses will be given by me.

> Sample sentence: I will give the twelve red roses.

_____

vii. Samuel will have his hair dyed gray by old age.

> Sample sentence: Old age will dye Samuel's hair gray.

_____

4. **SUMMARY**—Remember to keep only the most important ideas. The rest of the writing can be done away with. Each of the five *W*s and one *H* should be answered in your summary.

   A. Read *Zenobia, Queen of Palmyra* again. Decide which idea is the main idea and circle or highlight it.

   B. Underline any words essential to telling the story. Use these words to tell the story briefly in your summary.

   C. Eliminate any extra details. These details might make the story more fun to read, but they aren't necessary for readers to understand the main idea.**D**

   D. Rewrite the story in exactly six sentences. **D**Strikeouts are indicated in the teacher's edition for your ease of use.

Zenobia, Queen of Palmyra

—adapted from *Historic Girls* by E.S. Brooks and
The Story of the Romans by H.A. Guerber

~~M~~~~any miles and many days' journey toward the rising sun, over seas and mountains and deserts—farther to the east than Rome or Constantinople or even Jerusalem and old Damascus—stand the ruins of a once mighty city. It is known as Palmyra, once one of the most beautiful cities in the world.~~

~~Nature and art combined to make it glorious. Like a glittering mirage out of the sand-swept desert arose its palaces and temples and grandly sculptured archways. It had aqueducts and monuments and~~

gleaming porticos with countless groves of palm trees and gardens full of flowers. It had wells and fountains, market and circus, and broad streets stretching away to the city gates and lined on either side with magnificent colonnades of rose-colored marble. Such was Palmyra in the year 250.

A boy of sixteen and a girl of twelve looked down from a balcony upon the beautiful Street of the Thousand Columns. Both were handsome and healthy. The boy was named Odaenathus and the girl was Zenobia. As they looked lazily on the crowds below, a sudden exclamation from the lad caused his companion to raise her flashing black eyes inquiringly to his face. "What troubles you, my Odaenathus?" she asked.

"There, there! Look there, Zenobia!" replied the boy excitedly. "Coming through the Damascus arch, the Romans have returned. We thought them to be in Emesa."

The girl's glance followed his guiding finger. She saw the bright April sun gleam down upon the standard of Rome, with its eagle crest and its S.P.Q.R. design beneath. There came a trumpet peal, and, swinging into the great Street of the Thousand Columns at the head of his light-armed legionaries, rode the centurion Rufinus.

"But why should the coming of the Roman so trouble you, my Odaenathus?" she asked. "We are neither Jew nor Christian that we should fear his wrath, but free Palmyreans who bend the knee neither to Roman nor Persian masters."

"Who will bend the knee no longer, be it ever so little, my cousin," exclaimed the lad hotly. "Yet see—who comes now?" he cried. At once the attention of the young people was turned in the opposite direction as they saw, streaming out of the great fortress-like courtyard of the Temple of the Sun, another hurrying crowd, the glint of weaponry in their hands.

Then young Odaenathus gave a cry of joy. "See, Zenobia; they come, they come!" he cried. "It is my father, Odaenathus, the chief of the lords of Palmyra. This day will we fling off the Roman yoke and become the true and unconquered lords of Palmyra. And I, too, must join them," he added.

But the young girl detained him. "Wait, cousin," she said. "Watch and wait. Your father will scarce attempt so brave a deed today, with these new Roman soldiers in our gates. Truly that isn't wise."

The boy broke out again. "They have seen each other," he said. "Both sides are pressing on!"

"Yes, and they will meet under this very balcony," said Zenobia. Moved both by interest and desire, the dark-eyed Syrian girl, to whom fear was never known, looked down upon the tossing sea of spears and lances and glittering shields and helmets that swayed and surged in the street below.

"So, Odaenathus!" said Rufinus, the tribune, reining in his horse and speaking in harsh and commanding tones. "Why do you greet me with all these armed followers?"

"Are my movements of such importance to the noble tribune that he must question a free leader of Palmyra as to the number and manner of his servants?" asked Odaenathus haughtily.

"Dog of a Palmyrean! Slave of a camel-driver!" said the Roman angrily. "Free, never! None are free but Romans."

"Have a care, O Rufinus," said the older Odaenathus boldly. "Choose wiser words if you would have peaceful ways. Palmyra will not tolerate any such slander of her foremost men."

"And Rome will not tolerate such men as you, traitor," said Rufinus. "Ay, traitor, I say," he repeated. "Strike!" At his word the short sword in the ready hand of the big foot soldier went straight into Odaenathus's chest. The chief of Palmyra fell dead in the street.

So sudden and so unexpected was the blow that the Palmyreans stood as if stunned, unable to comprehend what had happened. But the Roman was swift to act.

"Sound, trumpets! Down, pikes!" he cried, and as the trumpet peal rose loud and clear, fresh soldiers came hurrying through the gate.

Before the lowered pikes could fully disperse the crowd, the throng parted and through the swaying mob there burst a lithe and flying figure—a brown-skinned maid of twelve with streaming hair, loose robe, and angry, flashing eyes. Right under the lowered pikes she darted and, flushed and panting, she defiantly faced the astonished Rufinus. Close behind her came an equally excited lad who, when he saw the stricken body of his father on the marble street, flung himself weeping upon it.

Zenobia's eyes flashed still more angrily. "Assassin, murderer!" she cried.

Lesson 9: *The Five Ws*

~~"You have slain my kinsman and Odaenathus's father. How dare you? How dare~~ ~~you!" she repeated vehemently, and then, flushing with deeper scorn, she added,~~ ~~"Roman, I hate you! Would that I were a man. Then should all Palmyra know how——"~~

~~"Whip these children home," broke in the stern Rufinus, "or fetch them by the~~ ~~ears to their nurses and their toys."~~

~~The struggling children were half led, half carried into the sculptured atrium of~~ ~~the palace of Odaenathus.~~ There under the vines and bowers of the garden, young Odaenathus and Zenobia swore eternal hatred for Rome.

Not long after, the kingdom of Palmyra gained in power and extent. The young Odaenathus became ruler and a strong war leader. He set about flexing the muscles of Palmyra by conquering Persia in the name of the Romans. Odaenathus then married Zenobia, and they had two children together. It seemed that they should have lived happily ever after, except that Zenobia still secretly hated bowing to Rome. Her husband warned her, "We have prospered under Rome. Let us forget our childish oath."

But then the young Odaenathus was also murdered by an assassin, and so Zenobia, his wife, governed in the name of her young son. ~~The young girl had~~ ~~grown into a beautiful and very able queen. She wished to rival Cleopatra in~~ ~~magnificence of attire and pomp, as well as in beauty.~~

Never tame in spirit, Zenobia took the title Empress of the East and tried to drive the Romans out of Asia forever. ~~In full armor, she led her troops into battle~~ ~~and conquered Egypt. She also entered into an alliance with the Persians. With~~ ~~the back of her kingdom secure, she set her sights on Asia Minor.~~

~~Meanwhile, Aurelian, the emperor of Rome, was forced to subdue the Goths~~ ~~before he could lead his legions against Zenobia. Eventually he marched the~~ ~~power and might of Rome against Palmyra. The queen of Palmyra was then~~ ~~defeated and her capital taken. Though she attempted to flee, she fell into the~~ ~~hands of the Romans. Many of Zenobia's most faithful supporters were killed.~~

~~Palmyra itself was at first spared, but the inhabitants revolted soon after~~ ~~the Romans had left. Aurelian therefore retraced his steps, took the city for the~~ ~~second time, and, after killing nearly all the people, destroyed both houses and~~

~~walls. Its wealth was so great that even the Romans were dazzled by the amount of gold they saw in Aurelian's triumph.~~

~~They also stared in wonder at~~ Zenobia, the proud eastern queen, who was forced to walk in front of Aurelian's chariot. ~~The unhappy woman could scarcely carry the weight of the priceless jewels she was forced to wear for the occasion.~~

~~When the triumph was over, Zenobia was allowed to live in peace and great comfort in a palace near Tibur, and there she brought up her children as if she had been only a Roman mother. Her daughters married Roman nobles, and one of her sons was given a small kingdom by the generous Aurelian.~~

Summary:

Sample summary: Odaenathus is the son of a Palmyrean chief, and Zenobia is his cousin. One day, they watch the Romans return to the city of Palmyra. The Palmyreans try to revolt, but Odaenathus's father, the chief, is murdered by the Romans. Odaenathus and Zenobia swear eternal hatred against the Romans. Zenobia takes the title Empress of the East and tries to drive the Romans out of Asia forever. Aurelian defeats Zenobia and parades her captive down the streets of Rome.

_____

_____

_____

_____

_____

_____

_____

_____

_____

_____

Speak It— 🎙️

With a partner, dramatically read to your class this adapted excerpt from William Ware's novel *Zenobia: The Fall of Palmyra*. Consider adding sound effects and wearing costumes or making a recording. Remember to read with volume, drama, gestures, and pauses. Try to demonstrate the character traits of your character with your voice.

Reader 1: Aurelian has arrived, and the long expected day has come and gone. His triumph over Palmyra has been celebrated, and with a magnificence and a pomp greater than the glories of Emperors Pompey, Trajan, Titus, or Philip.

Reader 2: We have seen Zenobia!

Reader 1: The sun of Italy never poured a flood of more golden light upon the great capital than on the day of Aurelian's triumph. The whole city was early abroad, and added to our own overgrown population there were the inhabitants of all the neighboring towns and cities and strangers from all parts of the empire, so that it was with difficulty, and no little danger too, that the spectacle could be seen. I found a position opposite the capitol from which I could observe the whole of this proud display of the power and greatness of Rome.

Reader 2: A long train of elephants opened the show, their huge sides and limbs hung with cloth of gold and scarlet. Some had upon their backs military towers, which were filled with the natives of Asia or Africa, all arrayed in the richest costumes of their countries. These were followed by wild animals and those remarkable for their beauty—lions, tigers, leopards—from every part of the world.

Reader 1: Then came not many fewer than 2,000 gladiators in pairs, all arranged in such a manner as to display to the greatest advantage their well-knit joints and swollen muscles. Of these a great number have already perished on the arena of the Flavian and in the sea fights in Domitian's theatre.

Reader 2: Next, upon gilded wagons and so arranged as to produce the most dazzling effect, came the spoils of the wars of Aurelian—treasures of art, rich cloths and embroideries, utensils of gold and silver, pictures, statues, and works in brass from the cities of Gaul, from Asia, and from Egypt. Conspicuous among this collection were the rich and gorgeous contents of the palace of Zenobia. The huge wagons groaned under the weight of vessels of gold and silver, of ivory and of the most precious woods of India. The jeweled wine cups, vases, and a golden sculpture of Demetrius attracted the gaze and excited the admiration of every beholder.

Reader 1: Immediately after these came a crowd of youths richly habited in the costumes of a thousand different tribes, bearing in their hands, upon cushions of silk, crowns of gold and precious stones, the offerings of the cities and kingdoms of all the world, as it were, to the power and fame of Aurelian.

Reader 2: Following these came the ambassadors of all nations, sumptuously arrayed in the habits of their respective countries. Then an innumerable train of captives, showing plainly in their downcast eyes, in their fixed and melancholy gaze, that hope had taken its departure from their breasts. Among these were many women from the shores of the Danube, taken in arms fighting for their country, of enormous stature and clothed in the warlike costume of their tribes.

Reader 1: But why do I detain you with these things, when it is of one only that you wish to hear? I cannot tell you with what impatience I waited for that part of the procession to approach that showed off Zenobia. I thought its line would stretch on forever. And it was the ninth hour before the alternating shouts and deep silence of the multitudes announced that the conqueror was drawing near the capitol.

Reader 2: All eyes were turned with pity upon Zenobia. No longer treated like a queen, she was now on foot and exposed to the rude gaze of the Roman populace, toiling beneath the rays of a hot sun. She was burdened with the weight of jewels such as, both for richness and beauty, were never before seen in Rome and with chains of gold, which, first passing around her neck and arms, were then borne up by attendant slaves. I could have wept to see her so—yes, and did.

Reader 1: My impulse was to break through the crowd and support her almost fainting form, but I well knew that my life would answer for the rashness on the spot. I could only, like the rest, wonder and gaze. And never did she seem to me, not even in the midst of her own court, to blaze forth with such transcendent beauty—yet she was touched with grief. Her look was not that of the dejection of one who was broken and crushed by misfortune; there was no blush of shame. It was rather one of profound, heartbreaking sadness.

Reader 2: When the emperor's pride had been sufficiently gratified, and when he came over against the steps of the capitol, he himself, crowned as he was with the diadem of universal empire, descended from his chariot and, unlocking the chains of gold that bound the limbs of the queen, led and placed her in her own chariot. It was not till the shades of evening had fallen that the last of the procession had passed the front of the capitol.

Lesson 9: The Five Ws

Talk About It—

1. Answers to the first question will vary. Fact-based questions such as "Who?", "What?", "When?", and "Where?" are often easier to answer than questions beginning with "why" and "how." "Why" and "how" questions can delve into the motives of a person or the cause of an event. For instance, if two cars crash, it's usually easy to say who was driving, what happened, when the wreck happened, and where it happened. But it's quite another thing to ask "why" and "how." Why did the wreck happen? Was it an accident or on purpose? How did the wreck happen? Was there a problem with the brakes or was the driver angry or did an egg hit the windshield? You must do more investigating to answer why and how.

2. Some people simply crave power—the freedom to do whatever they want. Other people want wealth and honor, while others may fight to free their people. Power can cause a person to be ruthless and to mistreat other people. It can cause people to be greedy. However, a good ruler can benefit his or her people by protecting them, by giving them useful laws to follow, and by punishing harmful people. Good character ensures that a leader's followers can trust him.

3. Zenobia is probably wondering what will become of Palmyra. Will the city be destroyed like Jerusalem or spared by the Romans? Will her people receive a wise or a cruel ruler? More than likely, she is sad to leave her home and her friends and all the familiar sights she loves so well. The setting sun in the background seems to indicate that her reign is also setting.

Notes

_____

_____

_____

_____

_____

_____

_____

_____

_____

_____

_____

_____

_____

_____

_____

_____

_____

_____

Lesson 10 ·

The Making of a Legend

Suppose an angler (fisherman) hooks a fish, but the fish, by thrashing and splashing, gets away. As the angler walks home with an empty bucket, she might exaggerate the size of her catch. To the first person she meets, she might describe the fish as a whopper, as long as her arm. To the second person she meets, she might describe the fish as bigger than her big brother. To the third person she meets, she might say the fish was nearly as big as her boat. To the fourth person she meets, she might say the fish was as big as a whale.

"Fish stories" such as this are called **legends**. A legend is a story that gets its start with a real person or a real event, but along the way it becomes exaggerated by storytellers. Did you notice how the story about the fish that got away became exaggerated the more times it was told? This is the way legends are made. They may only be slightly exaggerated or hugely exaggerated. It all depends on the honesty of the storytellers and how often the story is passed along.

To illustrate how a real life story can become a legend, try playing the familiar game of Telephone. All of the players should sit or stand side-by-side in a line. The person at one end of the line should think of a complex sentence such as, "Now is the time for every good man to come to the aid of his country." The sentence should be whispered to the next person in line and so on, passed along by whispering until it reaches the end of the line and everyone has heard it. The person at the end of the line gets to speak the sentence out loud. Has the sentence changed from the original? The more people there are in line, the more likely the sentence will be changed.

This next sentence about Davy Crockett, the American backwoodsman, is undoubtedly a truthful statement: "When he was just a boy, Davy Crockett killed a bear with his flintlock rifle." Davy encountered bears all the time in the wilderness of Tennessee. But by changing a few words at a time, the sentence can be made to sound more and more like a legend. Let's start with the first part, "When he was just a boy" and change it to, "When he was only three." That exaggerates the sentence quite a bit, doesn't it? How many three-year-olds do you know with the strength to hunt down a bear? If you were a storyteller, you'd certainly have the ears of your listeners.

What if you were to change the end of the sentence, "with his flintlock rifle," next? Can you think of a way to exaggerate this part of the sentence? How about by substituting "by hugging him to death"? Now the sentence reads: "When he was only three, Davy Crockett killed a bear by hugging him to death."

A teller of tall tales might even change the type of animal and the number of them that Davy Crockett killed. For instance: "When he was only three, Davy Crockett killed five alligators by hugging them to death."

There! Now the original sentence about a man who really lived and an event that really happened has been completely turned into a legend.

Now turn your attention to a young Roman soldier who became a popular legendary figure during the Middle Ages, Saint George. We know almost nothing about the life of Saint George except that he lived in the late third century and was killed during the persecution of Christians by the Roman emperor Diocletian. When you read his story, ask yourself what might be real (nonfiction) and what might be imaginary (fiction/legend).

Using a highlighter, mark any event in *Saint George and the Dragon* that seems to be an exaggeration or legendary to you. In other words, what do you think is real (nonfiction) and what do you think is imaginary (fiction)?

Lesson 10: The Making of a Legend

A Saint George is claimed as the patron or helper saint of many current nation-states and cities, including Georgia, Russia, England, Portugal, Brazil, and Malta. Cappadocia is a region in Asia Minor, today's Turkey.

nonfiction/factual

fiction/legendary

Saint George and the Dragon

—adapted from *Heroes Every Child Should Know* by Hamilton Wright Mabie **A**

In the year AD 280, in a town in Cappadocia, was born that great soldier and champion of the oppressed whom we call Saint George. His parents were Christians, and by them, and especially by his mother, he was most carefully instructed and trained. Ever since he was a young boy, he showed a desire to help people and to stand up to bullies.

When the youth came to the age of seventeen years, he took up the profession of arms, and since he was gifted with beauty of person, intelligence, and an exquisite courtesy, he rose rapidly to a considerable military rank. Especially he pleased his imperial master, the emperor Diocletian.

From the first, however, the young soldier George was angered by the cruelties put upon Christians, and he spoke out boldly in their defense. His friends counseled silence and **prudence**, but George could not remain silent. He knew that he might be called upon to suffer at any time, and he hoped to do better work for the world than die

What is a saint anyway? Today, when we say somebody is a saint, we usually mean that he or she is a good person. "Pedro is a saint because he's so patient." "Erica is a saint because she helps the elderly." "Saint" actually means "sanctified person" or "holy person," which is like saying "good" but with a healthy dose of religious devotion. In early Christian history, saints were people who were willingly martyred (killed) rather than give up their faith. The word later came to mean anybody who was especially devoted to God and lived a virtuous life. In the Middle Ages, saint stories were especially popular. Saints were like superheroes who did amazing deeds and miracles, and these stories inspired people to live better lives in a very rough and dangerous period of history. All religions have saints or people who are respected for their spiritual devotion. Saints are still cropping up in the modern world. Consider the life of Mother Teresa, who worked with the poorest of the poor in the slums of Calcutta, or Nelson Mandela, whose activism brought an end to apartheid in South Africa.

helplessly in the Roman arena. He therefore gave away his money and his fine clothes among the poor and needy, set free all the slaves he possessed, and went forth upon knightly travel.

While riding one day through the plains of Libya he came to a certain city called Silene. There, the people were bewailing a dire misfortune that had come upon them. An enormous dragon had issued from a marsh neighboring the town and had devoured all their flocks and herds. Already the monster had taken dwelling near the city walls, and at such distance the people had been able to keep him only by granting him two sheep every day for his food and drink. If they had failed in this he would have come within their walls and poisoned every man, woman, and child with his plague-like breath.

But now all the flocks and herds had been eaten. Nothing remained to satisfy the **insatiable** appetite of the dragon but the little people of the homes and hearths of all the town. Every day two children were now given him. All children under the age of fifteen were taken and chosen by lot. Thus it happened that every house and every street and all the public squares echoed with the wailing of unhappy parents and the cries of the innocents who were soon to be offered.

Lesson 10: The Making of a Legend

Now it chanced that the king of the city had one daughter, an exceedingly fair girl both in mind and body, and after many days of the choosing of lots for the sacrifice, and after many a blooming girl and boy had met an unhappy death, the lot fell to this maiden, Cleolinda. When her father, the king, heard his misfortune, in his despair he offered all the gold in the state treasury and even half his kingdom to redeem the maiden. But at this many fathers and mothers who had lost their children murmured greatly and said, "O king, art thou just? By thy edict thou hast made us desolate. And now behold thou wouldst withhold thine own child!"

Thus the people spoke, and speaking they grew very angry, and so joining together they marched, threatening to burn the king in his palace unless he delivered the maiden to fulfill her lot. To such demands the king submitted, and at last he asked only a delay of eight days that he might spend with his beloved girl and bewail her fate. This the people granted.

At the end of the time agreed, the fair victim was led forth. She fell at her father's feet asking his blessing and protesting that she was ready to die for her people. Then amid tears and lamentations she was led to the walls and put without. The gates were shut and barred against her.

She walked toward the dwelling of the dragon, slowly and painfully, for the road was strewn with the bones of her playmates, and she wept as she went on her way.

It was this very morning that George, courageously seeking to help the weak, being strong to serve the truth, was passing by in his knightly journeying. **B** He saw stretched before him the disgusting path, and, moved to see so beautiful a maiden in tears, he checked his charger and asked her why she wept. The whole pitiful story she recounted, to which the valiant one answered, "Fear not! I will deliver you."

"Oh noble youth," cried the fair victim, "tarry not here lest you perish with me. Fly, I beg you."

The idea of monsters, such as dragons and werewolves, is as old as time itself. In the ancient world and the Middle Ages, much of the world was still being discovered. The world was full of strange creatures that were spotted on the sea or in forests at night. Any unfamiliar creature might pass into legend as a monster. Monsters were often symbols of evil that could be conquered by the spiritual power of a saint.

"God forbid that I should fly," said George in answer. "I will lift my hand against this loathsome thing, and I will deliver you through the power that lives in all true followers of Christ."

At that moment the dragon was seen coming forth from his lair half flying and half crawling toward them. "Fly, I beseech you, brave knight," cried the fair girl, trembling. "Leave me here to die."

But George answered not. Rather he put spurs to his horse and, calling upon his Lord, rushed toward the monster. After a terrible and prolonged combat, he pinned the mighty hulk to the earth with his lance. Then he called to the maiden to bring him her belt. With this he bound the dragon fast and gave the end of the belt into her hand, and the subdued monster crawled after them like a dog.

Walking in this way they approached the city. All the onlooking people were stricken with terror, but George called out to them saying, "Fear nothing. Only believe that I have conquered this adversary, and I will destroy him before your eyes."

Then George slew the dragon and cut off his head, and the king gave great treasure to the knight. But all the rewards George distributed among the sick and needy and kept nothing for himself, and then he went further on his way of helpfulness.

According to legend, George was martyred in the **persecutions** against Christians that swept all across the Roman Empire under Diocletian.^C George is said to have been stretched to death on a wheel of sharp spokes or killed in a cauldron of boiling lead. Most likely, he was beheaded in April of the year AD 303.

B A knight-errant (or a traveling, wandering knight) was a popular figure in medieval literature. These knights went on missions of heroic deeds. Saint George was the perfect knight-errant because he was pious, brave and he saved a woman's life. Chivalric literature is sometimes cited as a significant cultural factor leading to the high station of women in today's west.

C The Diocletianic persecution was the sharpest and most widespread of the persecutions against Christians in the history of the Roman Empire. Christians were told to make sacrifices to the Roman gods. Those who refused often lost their lives. Legend is known to embellish certain aspects of a story including, but not limited to, the hyperbolic aspects of a saint's martyrdom.

Lesson 10: The Making of a Legend

Tell It Back — Narration

1. Oral narration: Without looking at the text, tell the legend of *Saint George and the Dragon* as best as you remember it using your own words. Try not to leave out any important detail. Here are the first two sentences to help you get started: "In the year AD 280, in a town in Cappadocia, was born that great soldier and champion of the oppressed whom we call Saint George. His parents were Christians, and by them, and especially by his mother, he was most carefully instructed and trained."

2. Outline: Create an outline for the legend *Saint George and the Dragon* using Roman numerals (*I, II, III*) for the most important events and capital letters (*A, B, C*) for less important events. Use standard numbers (*1, 2, 3*) for minor points.

Sample outline:
I. George's early life
   A. He is born in Cappadocia to Christian parents.
   B. He serves as a soldier in Roman army under Diocletian.
II. George becomes a knight errant.
   A. A dragon terrorizes town.
      1. The town is Silene in Libya.
      2. The dragon eats flocks.
      3. The dragon eats children second.
      4. The king's daughter will be the next to die.
   B. George rescues the princess.
      1. He cuts off the dragon's head.
      2. He receives a reward and gives it to the poor.
III. George is martyred.
   A. He is killed in the terrible persecution of Diocletian
   B. George is brutally killed:
      1. Wheel with sharp spokes
      2. Boiling lead
      3. Beheaded

_____

_____

_____

_____

_____

_____

_____

_____

_____

3. Written narration:

    a. Write your own sentence to tell what happens at the beginning of the story.

          Sample sentence: To escape death in the arena, George goes out into the world.

         _____

         _____

    b. Write your own sentence to tell what happens in the middle of the story.

          Sample sentence: George rescues a princess and her town by slaying a dragon.

         _____

         _____

    c. Write your own sentence to tell what happens at the end of the story.

          Sample sentence: George is killed during the persecutions of Diocletian.

         _____

         _____

Lesson 10: The Making of a Legend

Talk About It—

TE 1. When Americans created legends about Davy Crockett, they were eager to have a hero emerge from the backwoods, a "king of the wild frontier." America was a new nation, and the wilderness was frightening to many townspeople. Davy Crockett's life, legends, and adventures gave everyone a laugh, gave them courage, and boosted their pride in their new nation. Why do you suppose legends were created by early Christian storytellers about the young Roman soldier, George?

TE 2. Examine the painting *Saint George and the Dragon* by Baroque painter Peter Paul Rubens. Why did the painter pose Saint George the way he did high on the horse and above the dragon? How would you describe the look on his face as he slays the fearsome dragon?

TE 3. What are some clues in the story that the people in the town of Silene are foolish?

▲ *Saint George and the Dragon* by Peter Paul Rubens

ᴅ This painting was created around 1605 and currently resides in Madrid, Spain. For a list of the many illustrations that demonstrate how this image has captured the Western imagination see: http://en.wikipedia.org/wiki/Saint_George_and_the_Dragon.

Go Deeper—

Circle or supply the correct answer(s):

1. Which sentence best tells the main idea of the story?
   a. Roman emperors were all wicked men.
   b. Saints were hard to kill.
   c. Never live near a marsh or a dragon.
   d. Wherever he went, George did good deeds.

Lesson 10: The Making of a Legend

2. The noun "persecution" has the same Latin root as the noun "pursuit." "Persecution" means "trouble and harm against someone because of his beliefs." "Pursuit" means "a chasing after someone." How are the words "persecution" and "pursuit" similar in their meaning?

> — Sample answer: Both words can imply hunting someone for some reason. Persecution can — be a pursuit, or "a chasing after," to hurt someone for what he believes.

3. _His friends counseled silence and prudence, but George could not remain silent._ George's friends were worried that he would get into trouble. They encouraged him to shut his mouth and have prudence. If the penalty for speaking out against the emperor and his persecution of the Christians was torture and death, what does the noun "prudence" likely mean?
   a. carefulness
   b. anger
   c. rudeness
   d. stupidity

 Use the word "prudence" in your own complete sentence.

> Sample sentence: Always use prudence when you cross the river on those slippery rocks.

"Prudence" comes from the Latin _prudentia_, meaning "wisdom, foresight, and caution."

4. _Nothing remained to satisfy the insatiable appetite of the dragon but the little people of the homes._ If the dragon was always hungry no matter how much he ate, the adjective "insatiable" probably means:
   a. smelly
   b. never satisfied
   c. gigantic
   d. poisonous

Lesson 10: The Making of a Legend

Use the word "insatiable" in your own complete sentence.

> Sample sentence: I have an insatiable appetite for pepperoni pizza.

"Insatiable" comes from the Latin word *insatiabilis*. The prefix *in-* means "not," and *satiabilis* means "fullness" or "satisfaction."

5. Circle the adjective that best describes Saint George. Find a sentence in the narrative that supports your answer and write it in the space provided.

cowardly   courageous

> Sample answer: "God forbid that I should fly," said George in answer. "I will lift my hand against this loathsome thing."

Writing Time— ⏲

1. **DICTATION**—Your teacher will read a little part of *Saint George and the Dragon* back to you. Please listen carefully! After your teacher reads once, she will read slowly again and include the punctuation marks. Your task will be to write down the sentences as your teacher reads them one by one.

> Modify according to student level.
>
> 💬 If they had failed in this he would have come within their walls and poisoned every man, woman, and child with his plague-like breath.
>
> 💬 "Oh noble youth," cried the fair victim, "tarry not here lest you perish with me. Fly, I beg you."

2. **SENTENCE PLAY—**

Ever since he was a young boy, he showed a desire to help people. Using this sentence as a model, fill out the following sentences.

a. Ever since she was a young girl, Samantha _____

Sample sentence: Ever since she was a young girl, Samantha loved tiger cubs.

b. Ever since he lost his wallet, _____

Sample sentence: Ever since he lost his wallet, Fred couldn't pay for his coffee.

c. Ever since she travelled to China, _____

Sample sentence: Ever since she travelled to China, she used chopsticks instead of a fork.

d. Ever since _____

Sample sentence: Ever since the pilot sang crazily, Claudia has refused to fly on airplanes.

_____, Claudia has refused to fly on airplanes.

e. Ever since _____

Sample sentence: Ever since he visited the fair, Marcellus has enjoyed eating cotton candy.

_____, Marcellus has enjoyed eating cotton candy.

3. **COPIOUSNESS—**You have seen that sentences become stronger, more vigorous and intense, when specific words are used. This is true whether the word is a noun, an adjective, or a verb. Always search your mind, and sometimes a thesaurus, for the very best word to use.

4. Underline the adjectives in the following sentences and make them more specific. The adjective does not need to be a synonym.

a. Bearded dragons make <u>nice</u> pets for lovers of reptiles.

Sample sentence: Bearded dragons make tame pets for lovers of reptiles.

_____

Lesson 10: The Making of a Legend

b. It was <u>mean</u> and <u>bad</u> for the harpies to steal Phineas's food.

Sample sentence: It was foul and dangerous for the harpies to steal Phineas's food.

c. Have a <u>good</u> voyage and <u>good</u> weather, too.

Sample sentence: Have a safe voyage and mild weather, too.

d. Today the grocer is selling <u>red</u> apples and <u>green</u> papayas.

Sample sentence: Today the grocer is selling crimson apples and delectable papayas.

Underline the common nouns in the following sentences and replace them with more specific nouns. Do not change the proper nouns.

e. During <u>the meal</u>, Agrippina served Claudius delicious <u>food.</u>

Sample sentence: During dinner, Agrippina served Claudius delicious pudding.

f. Little did Claudius know, he had eaten bad <u>stuff.</u>

Sample sentence: Little did Claudius know, he had eaten bad mushrooms.

g. Claudius died late in the <u>day</u> and Nero became the new <u>leader.</u>

Sample sentence: Claudius died late in the afternoon and Nero became the new emperor.

h. Before long, Nero sank his own _relative_, Agrippina, in a _vessel_. **E**

> Sample sentence: Before long, Nero sank his own mother, Agrippina, in a boat.

5. Underline the state-of-being verbs in the following sentences and replace them with action verbs. Change the sentence as needed so that it makes sense.

   a. Josephina _is_ in the backyard.

   > Sample sentence: Josephina dances in the backyard.

   b. This afternoon, Winnie the Pooh _will be_ in his tree trunk eating honey.

   > Sample sentence: This afternoon, Winnie the Pooh will rest in his tree trunk eating honey.

   c. The tornado _was_ like a wild animal as it roared for dinner.

   > Sample sentence: The tornado twisted like a wild animal as it roared for dinner.

   d. The queen of fashion, Marie Antoinette _is_ in a gold and purple dress.

   > Sample sentence: The queen of fashion, Marie Antoinette, swaggers in a gold and purple dress.

6. Replace the dull nouns, adjectives, and verbs in the following sentence and create several new and exciting sentences.

   The _big_, _terrible_ _thing_ _ate_ my _stuff_ and _drank_ some _liquid_.

   a. > Sample sentences:
      >
      > The enormous, ferocious crocodile gobbled my books and gulped some chocolate milk.
      >
      > The huge, horrendous bear chewed my leg and swallowed some pond water.

b. _____

c. _____

> **E** The pursuit of power often takes many twists and turns. Agrippina is said to have poisoned her third husband, Claudius, in order to secure the throne for her son, Nero. In turn, Nero tried several times to murder his own mother, including an attempt to sink a pleasure boat she was riding in. And, of course, Nero was forced to commit suicide after his disastrous reign. While these are fascinating tidbits from history, they are not necessary to answering the questions in this section.

_____

7. AMPLIFICATION—

A. Dialogue: Write a dialogue to show what might have been said between George and the king after George rescued the town. Remember that dialogue is a conversation between two or more people.

> Sample dialogue: The king heaped jewels and precious metals—gold, silver, and platinum—at George's feet. "Sir knight," he said humbly, "I could not give you enough if I gave you all my kingdom to pay for the life of my daughter."
>
> George bowed, but he did not desire the king's praise. "Thank you, oh king, for these wondrous treasures. I will be sure to give them to the poor and the needy. But as for the life of your daughter, I did only my duty. How could I go on living with my conscience if I had let that loathsome beast devour her? And now I must carry on, good king. Adieu."

_____

_____

_____

_____

_____

_____

_____

_____

_____

_____

Lesson 10: The Making of a Legend

B. Description: Write a description of the terrible dragon. You may wish to describe the image of the dragon in *Saint George and the Dragon* by Armand Point or the painting by the same name by Paolo Uccello. Be sure to give details that appeal to all of the senses: sight, sound, smell, taste, and touch.

▲ *Saint George and the Dragon* by Armand Point

▲ *Saint George and the Dragon* by Paolo Uccello

Sample description: The dragon had scales that were as large as gold dollars and the color of the kind of murky water that makes it impossible to see the bottom of a lake. When it walked, it heaved its enormous and dangerous tail after it. The air around the dragon for about 100 feet smelled like sulfur, an aftereffect of the flames it shot out of its mouth. When it walked, the ground shuddered, as if it, too, were afraid of what would come next. The dragon's sharp teeth were especially frightening because they looked like they could rip a human being from head to toe without much effort at all.

Please keep in mind that amplification is not always achieved by exaggeration. Amplification means to enlarge by detail, description, or dialogue. For example, "the pretty butterfly" becomes "the gold-and-blue butterfly flitting from daisy to daisy." Exaggeration means an overstatement of the facts. "The pretty butterfly" then becomes "the butterfly with colors more dazzling than a rainbow." Amplification does not always use exaggeration.

Lesson 10: The Making of a Legend

C. The following is a summary from a Roman work of fiction known as *The Satyricon*, believed to have been written by Petronius. Rewrite the paragraph to make it more exaggerated. Use your imagination to come up with even more spectacular supper dishes.

A rich plebeian named Trimalchio is fond of throwing parties. In his gorgeous house are four vast banqueting halls. His bees come from Greece, and his mushrooms are gathered in India. He owns estates and mansions that he has never seen. Now he gives a dinner for his hundred guests. For one course, every dish resembles a sign of the Zodiac. Then follows a boar, served whole, with baskets of sweetmeats hanging from his tusks. A huntsman stabs the boar, and out of its belly fly live birds, which are caught in nets as they fly about the room. Then the ceiling opens, and down comes a great tray filled with fruits and desserts. The meal is accompanied by singing, dancing, instrumental music, and floods of wine.**F**

Sample amplification: A huntsman stabs the roast boar, and out of its belly emerges five dancing dwarves, each holding a tray brimming with fruit: grapes, cherries, and honeydew melon. And so on.

F Sweetmeats are sugary confections and candied fruit.

_____

_____

_____

_____

_____

_____

_____

_____

_____

8. **REWRITE**— Change the underlined portions of the following sentences to make them sound more exaggerated and legendary.[G]

a. Hrothgar, king of the Danes, built a great hall with <u>a roof as high as the branches of trees</u>.[H]

> Sample sentence: Hrothgar, king of the Danes, built a great hall with a roof as high as the flight of an eagle.

b. In deadly pain, Roland blew his horn so loudly that <u>his eardrums burst</u>.[I]

> Sample sentence: In deadly pain, Roland blew his horn so loudly that his lips blew off his mouth.

c. Bravely, Nicolette entered the dark forest, not afraid of <u>the tusks of wild boars or the teeth of wolves</u>.[J]

> Sample sentence: Bravely, Nicolette entered the dark forest, not afraid of the fangs of werewolves or the nip of vampire bats.

d. Charlemagne was a very tall man for his time, and his foot was <u>exactly twelve inches long</u>.[K]

> Sample sentence: Charlemagne was a very tall man for his time, and his foot was exactly one yard long.

Speak It—The Greetings Game

This exercise makes use of improvisation (or improv), which is a form of spontaneous speaking or acting. Students will be chosen in pairs to come to the front of the class. The teacher will ask the first pair to greet each other and shake hands in the ordinary way that people say hello. Then the teacher will ask the same pair to greet each other in a very specific way, seeking to exaggerate everything that happens. Then another pair will take a turn.

Lesson 10: The Making of a Legend

This chapter focuses on the way hyperbole and exaggeration make their way naturally into stories that are retold, especially those retold in the oral tradition. Exaggeration happens naturally when we seek to impersonate a certain type of person. Watch what happens when you improvise in this exercise.

Some scenarios for exaggeration include:

- greeting like two cowboys or cowgirls
- greeting like two hula-hoop experts
- greeting like two peg-legged pirates
- greeting like two people with bad breath
- greeting like two flowery poets
- greeting a long-lost friend
- a greeting between a private and a general
- a greeting between two bullies
- a greeting between two boring people
- greeting someone who has a secret crush on you
- a greeting with a hug in which one girl spoils the other's makeup

G It might be good to remind students how oral telling and retelling can change and exaggerate the details of a story. At the same time, oral stories can remain very stable, such as when tribes use, in essence, professional storytellers to remember the deeds of the past. *Beowulf*, from which one of the following sentences was taken, may have been part of that oral tradition until it was written down by a monk/poet in early medieval times.

H In the epic *Beowulf*, Hrothgar's mead hall is described as a palace, although it was probably not much bigger than a couple of good-sized barns.

I The "Song of Roland" tells us that Roland's temples burst from the strain of blowing his horn.

J "Aucassin and Nicolette" is one of the most delightful love stories told by minstrels in the Middle Ages.

K Charlemagne's famous foot became the standard measure of a foot everywhere.

Lesson 10: *The Making of a Legend*

Lesson 10: The Making of a Legend

Talk About It—

1. Christians wanted to hold onto their faith despite the terrible things that were happening to them. Martyrs like George were heroes who would not let go of their faith even when faced with torture, and their stories encouraged the survivors. Legends like the story of the dragon were a way to say, "We are not helpless. We will go on doing good even when people hate us and want us dead."

2. Rubens positioned George above the dragon to show that George was in control of the situation, and the look on his face shows no fear. At the same time, George does not look pleased that he has to slay the creature, but he is willing to do the deed to save the princess.

3. It's not clear why the king doesn't simply order his people to abandon the town or why the people themselves don't run away. It also seems strange that the people of Silene don't try to attack the beast themselves.

Notes

The purpose of this lesson is to give students a springboard into writing their own stories based on historical fact and setting. In doing so they will practice all the skills learned in previous chapters.

Lesson 11 ···

Write Your Own Story— Historical Fiction

Have you ever written a story of your own? Do you enjoy writing stories? Many people find writing to be one of the happiest pursuits of their lives. Using your imagination, you can create whole new worlds such as Oz or Narnia or Middle Earth. You can create characters who seem almost to come alive, such as Tom Sawyer or Anne Shirley or Brer Rabbit. It's no wonder that some people dedicate their entire lives to writing.

▶In the first lesson, you learned about two important parts of a story. Do you remember what every story must have?

1. Every story must have a beginning, a middle, and an end. This is the plan or plot of a story.

2. Every story must have a character or characters. These are the persons, animals, or things that have different roles in the story. The main character is called the protagonist, and the conflict-causing character is called the antagonist.

You are now going to write a fiction set during the days of the Roman Empire. This type of story is called "historical fiction" because it is a make-believe story, but it takes place in a real historical setting. More than likely, you've already read historical fiction. Books such as *Little House on the Prairie*, The Roman Mysteries, *Caddie Woodlawn*, and *Sounder* are examples of fictional stories set in the past.

Read the following three stories to gather ideas for your Roman tale. Then, choose one of the three story scenarios (indicated by ) and follow the steps listed in the "Preparing Your Story" section.

Barbarian Invasion Story

—adapted from *Historical Tales: Roman* by Charles Morris and *The Story of the Romans* by H.A. Guerber

The doom of Rome was at hand. Its empire had extended almost without limit to the east and west, had crossed the sea and deeply penetrated the desert to the south, but had failed in its advances to the north. The Rhine and the Danube Rivers here formed its boundaries. The great forest region, which lay beyond these, with its hosts of blue-eyed and fair-skinned barbarians, defied the armies of Rome. Here and there the forest was penetrated and hundreds of thousands of its tenants were slain, yet Rome failed to subdue its swarming tribes. Early in the history of Rome it was taken and burnt by the Gauls. Raids of barbarians across the border were frequent in its later history. As Rome grew weaker, the tribes of the north grew bolder and stronger. The armies of the empire were kept busy holding the lines of the Rhine and the Danube. At length weak rulers and civil wars permitted this barrier to be broken, and the beginning of the end was at hand.

During the reign of Decius, a fierce race of barbarians called Goths came sweeping down from the north. They were tall and fierce and traveled with their wives and children, their flocks, and all they owned.

The Goths were divided into two large tribes: the Ostrogoths, or East Goths, and the Visigoths, or West Goths. All these barbarians spoke a rough Teutonic dialect like the one from which the present German language has grown, and among the gods they worshiped was Odin.

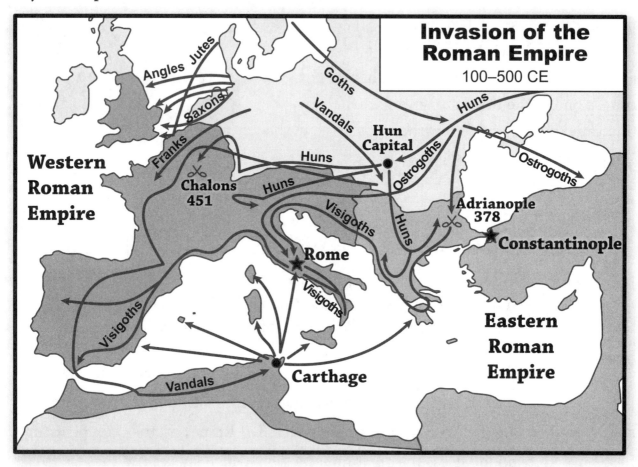

Write a story about a girl or boy caught in a Roman town that is being surrounded and attacked by a horde of Goths. Do some research on the appearance, apparel, and weapons of the Goths. Will your protagonist find a way to rescue the town? Will your protagonist escape the walls of the city? Will your protagonist be able to warn the Roman garrison fifty miles distant?

Gladiator Story

See page 181 for note A.

—adapted from *Historical Tales: Roman* by Charles Morris
and *The Story of the Romans* by H.A. Guerber **A**

The gladiators were first heard of in 264 BC, when their shows were given only at funerals. Usually they were criminals or prisoners of war who, in any case, were condemned to death. To give them arms and make them fight until one or the other was killed in the arena of some great building, for the amusement of a crowd of spectators, was cruel, but not so cruel as what was done in later years.

The shows of the gladiators came to please the people so well that they forsook theatres and other places of amusement. Rich citizens who wished to win the favor of the people began to keep bands of gladiators and train them as in a school. Citizens who kept these schools vied with one another to find the most powerful and muscular barbarians, for the stronger and better trained the gladiator the more exciting and pleasing to the people was the show. So the unfortunate men who were forced to slaughter one another for the amusement of the people were not criminals already condemned to death, but rather innocent men.

Many gladiators were killed in the arenas and amphitheaters of the Romans. Of these, the most impressive and deadly was the Colosseum, completed in AD 80 by Emperor Titus.

Nothing was omitted in the Colosseum that could add to the pleasure and convenience of the spectators. A canopy, drawn over their heads, protected them from the sun and the rain. Fountains refreshed the air with cooling moisture, and aromatics profusely perfumed the air. In the center was the arena, or stage, strewn with fine sand and capable of being changed to suit varied spectacles. One moment it appeared to rise out of the earth, like the gardens of the Hesperides; the next it was made to represent the rocks and caverns of Thrace. Water was abundantly supplied by concealed pipes, and the sand-strewn plain might at will be converted into a wide lake, sustaining armed vessels and displaying the swimming monsters of the deep.

💡 Write a story about a gladiator in training and do some research on gladiators. What is it like to learn how to use weapons for deadly combat? What doubts does your character, a new gladiator, feel about hurting other people for sport? What happens when he fights in the arena? Does he kill his opponent, or does he show mercy? Use your imagination to write an exciting tale.

💡 Do you remember the story of Androclus from lesson 4? Stories about lions befriending men by having thorns removed from their paws can be attributed to ancient fables. Using the following summary for inspiration, write out your own story of a boy or girl who rescues an animal and who is, in turn, rescued by that animal in the Roman amphitheater. Animals used for entertainment included bears, tigers, leopards, antelopes, ostriches, wild horses, and bulls. Add details such as dialogue and description that will make your story more interesting.

Androclus and the Lion

(This is one of a number of variations of the story of Androclus.)

A slave named Androclus once escaped from his master and fled to the forest. As he was wandering about there, he came upon a lion lying down, moaning and groaning. At first he turned to flee, but finding that the lion did not pursue him, he turned back and went up to him. As he came near, the lion put out his paw, which was swollen and bleeding, and Androclus found that a huge thorn had got into it and was causing all the pain. He pulled out the thorn and bound up the paw of the lion, who was soon able to rise and lick the hand of Androclus like a dog. Then the lion took Androclus to his cave and every day brought him meat from which to live.

Shortly afterward both Androclus and the lion were captured, and the slave was sentenced to be thrown to the lion after the lion had been kept without food for several days. The emperor and all his court came to see the spectacle, and Androclus was led out into the middle of the arena. Soon the lion was let loose from his den and rushed bounding and roaring toward his victim. But as soon as he came near to Androclus, he recognized his friend and fawned upon him, licking his hands like a friendly dog. The emperor, surprised at this, summoned Androclus to him, who told him the whole story, whereupon the slave was pardoned and freed and the lion let loose to his native forest.

Preparing Your Story

1. Circle your choice of names for your protagonist and your antagonist(s) from the following list of Roman names.

Roman Girl Names

Antonia	Faustina	Lucia
Barbara	Flavia	Marcella
Camilla	Julia	Matidia
Cecilia	Lara	Priscilla
Fabiola	Lavinia	Virginia

▲ Gladiators were captives or slaves who were trained to be professional fighters for the entertainment of Roman crowds. In many ways, they were like the boxers of today, although gladiatorial combats almost always ended in death. Each gladiator carried different types of weapons and were called by names according to their uniform: Thracian, hoplomachus, murmillo, and retiarius.

Roman Boy Names

Aquila	Felix	Justin
Augustus	Gaius	Lucas
Claudius	Hadrian	Marcus
Cornelius	Horace	Octavius
Fabian	Julius	Valerius

2. Fill out the following character survey for your protagonist.

My New Character

a. Full name:

_____

b. Male or female?

_____

c. Race or ethnicity:

_____

d. Age in years:

_____

e. Age description (circle): baby, toddler, kid, tween, teenager, young adult, adult, senior, elder

f. Height and weight in numbers:

_____

g. Height and weight description (circle): short, squat, small, puny, tiny, delicate, tall, hulking, lanky, lean, skinny, wiry, angular, slender, medium, trim, brawny, beefy, burly, sturdy, slim, spare, stout, stocky, big, portly, chubby, fat, pudgy

h. Hair and eye color:

_____

i. Hair description (circle): straight, curly, wavy, kinked, spiky, soft, velvety, springy, thick, frizzy, short, long, ropy, shaved, bald

j. Eye description (circle): round, narrow, almond, puffy, droopy, bleary, red, tired, heavy, deep, dancing, flashing, glinting, sparkling, twinkling, stony

k. Distinct physical traits such as voice, health, size of nose, missing limbs or eyes, glasses, moles, warts, or wrinkles

_____

_____

Lesson 11: Write Your Own Story—Historical Fiction

Character Quirks (oddities of behavior)

a. Odd tastes in clothing:

_____

b. Style of walking or talking:

_____

c. Eating habits or tastes:

_____

d. Good habits:

_____

e. Bad habits:

_____

Character Occupation

What does your character do for a living? Some Roman occupations include: actor, architect, artist, mosaic maker, baker, barber, weaver, brewer, butcher, carpenter, perfume maker, olive oil seller, centurion, foot soldier, gladiator, equestrian (cavalry officer), glassblower, clothing dyer, slave, courier (message runner), bathhouse worker, innkeeper, farmer, fisherman, fishmonger (fish seller), peddler, merchant, sailor, philosopher, teacher, student, librarian, physician, priest, shepherd, consul, tribune, senator, magistrate, tax collector.

_____

Character Adjectives

3. Use adjectives to describe your character. Remember that a protagonist should have some likeable qualities. Here are a few to consider: cheerful, lazy, shy, proud, polite, lonely, friendly, silly, bossy, grumpy, gentle, loving, messy, stupid, brave, clumsy, sneaky, saintly, innocent, sweet.

_____

4. Use two sentences to answer each of the five Ws and one H.

   a. Who is the main character of your narrative?

   _____

   _____

   _____

   b. What is the main event or action of your narrative?

   _____

   _____

   _____

   c. When does your narrative take place?

   _____

   _____

   _____

   d. Where does your narrative take place?

   _____

   _____

   _____

e. How does your protagonist overcome his or her antagonist? In other words, how is the conflict resolved?

_____

_____

_____

f. Why are you telling this particular story?

_____

_____

_____

5. Make your story more believable by giving it details from history. Circle at least six of the following words to use in your story.

amphora (oval vase with handles)

aqueduct

avia (grandmother)

avus (grandfather)

baths (bathhouse)

bishop

catacomb

centurion

chariot

Circus Maximus (ancient Roman chariot racing stadium)

citizen

coliseum (amphitheater)

colonnade

Colosseum (in Rome)

column

domus (house)

emperor

frater (brother)

gladiator

gladius (short sword)

gymnasium

insula (apartment)

legionary

mater (mother)

milestone

mosaic

oil lamp

pagan

Pantheon

pater (father)

patricians

Pax Romana (time of peace)

plebeians

scroll

slave

soror (sister)

stola (woman's dress)

stylus (pen)

temple

Tiber River

toga

tunic

Via Appia (Roman road)

villa

6. Think about where to begin your story and where to end it. Jot down your ideas in the space provided.

- Beginning

_____

_____

_____

_____

_____

_____

_____

_____

- Ending

_____

_____

_____

_____

_____

_____

_____

_____

Lesson 11: Write Your Own Story—Historical Fiction

Outline the major points of your story using Roman numerals (*I, II, III*) for the most important events and capital letters (*A, B, C*) for less important events. Use standard numbers (*1, 2, 3*) for minor points.

_____

_____

_____

_____

_____

_____

_____

_____

_____

_____

_____

_____

_____

_____

_____

_____

_____

_____

Lesson 11: Write Your Own Story—Historical Fiction

Elocution Instructions

Whether you are reciting a poem or reading a story out loud, you want to speak in such a way that your audience can hear you "loud and clear." The art of speaking skillfully is known as elocution. So, what goes into proper elocution?

First of all, you should make sure you are pronouncing all of your words clearly. This means you are making each word sharp and crisp instead of blending them together and mumbling. You want to say, "A bull once treading near a bog," with each word separate from the next. You don't want to say, "Abulloncetreadingnearabog."

Second, good posture is very important for speaking loudly enough. You can't breathe very well if you are slouched over. Stand up straight and tall, square your shoulders, and look at your audience. Look directly into their eyes. This will help your listeners know that you are a confident speaker. They will enjoy your recitation more when they see how confident you are.

Finally, don't speak too quickly. It's hard to understand a recitation that blasts off like a rocket ship. You will want to speak at a good pace and pause every now and then to let your words sink in.

In addition, practice speaking with

- volume. Everyone in the room should be able to hear you.
- drama. You should sound sad when the words call for sorrow, angry when the words call for anger. Any emotion in the text should find its way into your voice.
- gestures. Gestures accentuate the emotions in your voice and make the reading even more dramatic.
- pauses and proper speed. Never read quickly without taking a breath. Pauses help to accentuate your emotions like gestures.

You will delight your listeners if you can stand up straight, look into their eyes, and speak loudly and clearly at just the right pace. As you practice speaking skillfully, your writing will be improved. And as your writing improves, your speaking will also improve—they work together.

Logos and *Lexis*

Ancient educators taught us nearly everything we know about rhetoric. Aristotle noted two important parts of rhetoric: *logos* and *lexis*. *Logos* is Greek for "word" and also for "logical reasoning." So *logos* is the content, the substance of a speech. It's what you put down on paper and the words that are spoken. *Lexis* is the delivery of the words, how the speech comes across to the audience.

Both *logos* and *lexis* are important for effective oration. We might call them substance and style today. The content of a speech can mean the difference between sharing excellent ideas or spouting stuff and nonsense. The way you use your voice in speaking can mean the difference between catching the interest of your audience or putting them to sleep.

What are some ways to make the delivery, or *lexis*, of a speech more interesting? You already know that proper volume—loudness and softness—is vital to *lexis*. Speed—not speaking too fast or too slowly—is also key. In addition to proper volume and speed, there is also inflection. What is inflection?

Think about the different ways you could say the words, "I'd like to have you for dinner." If you say this sentence in a nice, casual voice, it sounds as if you are inviting someone to your house for a meal. If you say it sarcastically, it sounds like you think someone eats like a pig. If you say it in a raspy, wolfish voice, it sounds as if you want to eat someone up. The change in the pitch or tone of your voice is called inflection.

In order to hold your audience's attention, you are going to need to use the highs and lows of your voice. Inflection tells the audience when they need to be excited or when they should laugh or get serious. We know that when a person asks us a question, his voice will get a little higher at the end of his sentence. We know when we're about to hear bad news because a person's voice goes lower. A good speaker will know how to use inflection to make his speech more powerful.

Glossary of Words in This Book

Literary and Rhetorical Concepts

Active voice—the subject does the action of the action verb (e.g., The spider ate the fly.)

Adjective—describes a noun and helps us to "see" it more clearly: e.g., happy, silly, strange

Amplification—a longer or more detailed version of a shorter story

Anthropomorphism—use of a storybook animal that acts like a human being[1]

Ballad—a song that tells a story

Character—a person that has a role to play in a story

Character traits—qualities that make a person unique

Conflict—a clash between people or ideas

Copiousness—stretching exercises for students of rhetoric whereby students reach for new words to express variations of the same idea[2]

Dialogue—a conversation between two or more people

Elocution—the art of public speaking

Eloquence—skillful and persuasive speech and writing

Fable—a short story that teaches a simple moral lesson, usually with talking animals

Fact—a truth, something known to exist or to have happened

Fairy tale—a fanciful story for children, usually with magical people or creatures

Fiction—any imaginary story

First person—uses the pronouns "I," "me," "my"; the narrator takes part in the story

History—a narrative of actual events

Hook—the attention grabber of a story

Inflection—the change in pitch or tone of the voice that is used to make spoken words more meaningful

Legend—a story that begins with a real person or event that, as it is handed down by storytellers, often gets exaggerated along the way

---

1. Of course, anthropomorphism goes beyond storybook animals acting like humans. Anything that is nonhuman but represented as having human qualities is an example of anthropomorphism in action. A machine or a storm, a house or a tree, can all be anthropomorphized.

2. A broad definition of copiousness is any large quantity or number. Food, birds, or bubbles can be copious. In rhetoric, copiousness is aimed at developing a richness and flexibility of language so that many words and many ways of phrasing those words are available to the writer and speaker.

Glossary of Words in This Book

Lexis—the manner of delivery of a speech

Logos—the content of a speech

Main idea—the most important thought in a story or speech; what the story or speech is all about

Memorize—to learn something by heart

Monologue—a long speech by one person or character

Moral—the short lesson that explains the meaning of a fable

Myth—an ancient story not based on actual events, with gods, goddesses, and heroes

Narrative—all forms of story, from fairy tale, to history, to myths, to parables, to fables

Nonfiction—a narrative based on fact

Noun—a person, place, thing, or idea: e.g., astronaut, island, sled, love

Opinion—a personal claim, not necessarily based on fact

Outline—the skeleton of a story that tells what comes in the beginning, the middle, and the end

Parable—a short story that teaches a moral lesson, always true to life

Passive voice—the subject is acted upon by the action verb (e.g., The fly was eaten by the spider.)

Plot—the plan of a story, the events that form the beginning, the middle, and the end

Point of view—a way of seeing things

Proper noun—names a specific person, place, thing, or idea: e.g., Henrietta, Spain, Kleenex

Proverb—a wise saying

Rhetoric—the art and practice of persuasive writing and speaking

Rhyme—similar sounds repeated close to each other in poetry

Simile—a comparison using the words "like" or "as"

Stanza—a section of poetry similar to a paragraph in prose

Subject—what the sentence is about

Summary—a shortened or concise version of a longer story

Synonym—a word that has nearly the same meaning as another word

Vocabulary—a collection of words

Vocabulary Builder

Alliance—a group or groups that are united to help each other in war and peace

Antagonist—the opposing character of a story

Atrium—the central room of a Roman house, open to the sky in the center

Coffer—treasure chest

Conceited—thinking too highly of oneself

Conflagration—a large, destructive fire

Contusion—bruise

Degrading—disgraceful

Devour—to eat greedily

Disaster—a terrible misfortune or a total failure

Disgust—a feeling of sickness or strong dislike

Dull—boring, not colorful, stupid, or lacking sharpness

Duplicitous—double-dealing and not to be trusted

Entrails—guts

Flammable—easy to set on fire or burn

Gullible—easily deceived or cheated

Immortal—anyone or anything that will not die

Insatiable—unable to be satisfied

Interred—buried

Lithe—bendable, flexible

Lupercal—a Roman festival

Martyr—someone who is killed for his beliefs

> **A** You may want to point out to students that the grapheme *æ* is pronounced like a long *e*. The word *prætor* is pronounced pree-ter.

Mirage—something that is seen and appears to be real but that is not actually there

Patrician—the highest class of Roman citizen

Persecution—trouble and harm against someone because of his beliefs

Plebeian—a member of the common people of ancient Rome

Plunder—stolen property, usually taken by force in war

Prætor—a Roman leader and government official, often with the power to judge **A**

Prodigious—extremely large or strong, wonderful

Prosperous—wealthy

Glossary of Words in This Book

Protagonist—the main character or hero of a story

Pursuit—a chasing after someone

Prudence—wisdom, foresight, and caution

Resolve—to clear up or solve; to make a firm decision

Scapegoat—a person or group who takes the blame for what others have done

Slander—false talk that tears a person down in an attempt to give him or her a bad reputation

Surge—a wavelike rush or swell

Toil—hard work

Wily—full of clever tricks

Wrath—extreme anger

Yoke—a device used to join draft animals, or animals that pull, like oxen and horses; also refers to a source of subjection or servitude

Farewell

What? What? Are we finished with another book so soon? *Tempus fugit!* Or, in plain English, time flies! I sure hope you had some fun along the way.

Even if writing isn't your favorite thing, even if you feel pummeled and bruised, and you need to dust off the seat of your pants, we would be surprised if you didn't tell us that you're a better writer now than before you got started. Not only that, you learned quite a lot.

You learned that story and a narrative mean the same thing, and that stories have a plot and characters. Stories are an essential tool of rhetoric, which is the art of speaking and writing persuasively. And then you learned that there are many types of stories, everything from fables to histories, legends, myths, parables, and ballads.

But we are not finished, not by a long shot! You also learned that *logos* is the content and substance of a speech whereas *lexis* is how a speech is delivered. Whenever you speak in public, you can really wow an audience with proper delivery or elocution. This includes standing up straight, looking confidently at the audience, speaking with proper volume, and using inflection. Inflection is the drama in your voice—the pitch and loudness—that makes your words interesting.

Why stop there? You learned how to outline the plot of a story. You learned how to write the beginning, middle, and end of a story, and now you know that every interesting story has conflict in the middle. Conflict! Isn't that when the protagonist, or the main character, tries to reach a goal, only to be frustrated by an antagonist? Yes, you are correct! Conflict is any kind of fight or battle or competition between the protagonist and the antagonist. You also learned that the five *W*s and one *H*—who? what? when? where? why? how?—can help you to tell a story.

Now we're quite out of breath. Next time we get together, in *Writing & Rhetoric Book IV: Chreia*, we'll introduce to you something that's quite different than a narrative. It's a special little essay called a *chreia*. But you'll just have to wait to hear more. This is what you call a story cliffhanger. . . . You are hanging by your fingernails on the edge of a cliff and we will leave you hanging there.

I bid you farewell. Until soon!

Notes

Narrative II Rubric

This is a rubric developed by teachers who have taught writing and rhetoric in a school setting, and it is designed according to the needs of their classrooms. As with every aid in this book, use it only if you find it to be helpful. Feel free to create your own rubric for grading these compositions or choose some other form of evaluation.

Educators should be careful not to disproportionately weight various parts of a rubric, as the result may punish a student for one weakness even when she shows various other strengths. Remember that you should be assessing your students based on what you have clearly taught them and not on the basis of an external standard.

Name: _____

Date of Assignment: _____

Content _____/90

Plot _____/40

Does the narrative have a clear beginning? (10 points) _____

Does the narrative have a clear middle? (10 points) _____

Does the narrative have a clear end? (10 points) _____

Are the questions *who*, *what*, *when*, *where*, *why*, and *how* answered? (10 points) _____

Character _____/10

Does the narrative have a protagonist? (5 points) _____

Does the narrative have an antagonist? (5 points) _____

Conflict _____/10

Does the narrative have a clear conflict between
the protagonist and antagonist? (10 points) _____

Dialogue & Descriptions _____/30

Is the story enhanced by dialogue? (10 points) _____

Does the narrative contain a description of the setting(s)
and the characters? (10 points) _____

Does the narrative make use of some historical elements? (10 points) _____

Form _____/10

Number of spelling errors _____

2 or fewer per page: 4 points

3–4 per page: 2 points

5 per page: 1 point

6 or more per page: 0 points

Number of punctuation/capitalization errors

    _____

2 or fewer per page: 4 points

3–4 per page: 3 points

5 per page: 2 point

6 or more per page: 0 points

Is the handwriting neat and legible?

    _____

Yes: 1 point

No: 0 points

Total: _____/100

Narrative II Rubric

A CREATIVE APPROACH TO THE CLASSICAL PROGYMNASMATA

Writing Rhetoric

BOOK 4: CHREIA & PROVERB

PAUL KORTEPETER

BOOK 4, CHREIA / PROVERB

Chreia: A brief reminiscence of a person reporting a useful saying or deed.
Proverb: A brief tribute to a pity saying, in Chreia form.

Students learn to write a 6 paragraph essay using the 5 W's: who, what where, why and how:
- Students write on a deed (Chreia) or saying (Proverb) of a noteworthy person
- Everything contextualized in the story: grammar, wordplay, comprehension, outlining, analogical thinking, sentence play
- Historical narrative about a person including King Arthur, King Alfred, Lady Godiva, Queen Elizabeth

The expectations for each paragraph are clear and natural in relation to the story:
- Praise the person—what he said or how he lived
- Restate the saying or deed
- What is useful about this deed or saying
- Give a contrasting example
- Make a comparison
- Conclude

CLASSICAL ACADEMIC PRESS
Classical Subjects Creatively Taught

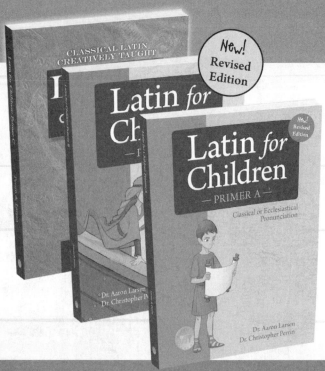